SUPPLEMENTAL EXERCISES TO ACCOMPANY

# *Foundations First*

## SENTENCES AND PARAGRAPHS

SECOND EDITION

SUPPLEMENTAL EXERCISES TO ACCOMPANY

# *Foundations First*

## SENTENCES AND PARAGRAPHS

SECOND EDITION

prepared by

*Judith Lechner*

*Carolyn Lengel*

**Bedford/St. Martin's**

Boston ■ New York

Manufactured in the United States of America.

9 8 7
f e d c

*For information, write:* Bedford/St. Martin's, 75 Arlington Street,
Boston, MA 02116 (617-399-4000)

ISBN: 0-312-41967-8

EAN: 978-0-312-41967-7

# *Preface for Instructors*

The exercises in this book are designed to provide additional practice for students using *Foundations First: Sentences and Paragraphs* by Laurie G. Kirszner and Stephen R. Mandell. The 93 exercise sets cover the grammar, punctuation, and mechanics topics in Units 3–6 of *Foundations First*.

Each grammar exercise is cross-referenced to the relevant section(s) of *Foundations First*, and exercises also available in electronic form (via the Exercise Central online collection) are so marked. Answers to all the exercises appear at the end of the book so that students can work independently.

Most of the exercise sets are written as connected discourse and have a thematic focus so that students are reading and revising ideas in context, rather than as isolated statements.

More exercise and test materials are available to *Foundations First* users in the following supplements:

- *Diagnostic and Master Tests to Accompany* *Foundations First* is a test book available to instructors.
- Exercise Central, an electronic exercise bank comprising nearly 7,000 items, is accessible to students and instructors via <bedfordstmartins.com/foundationsfirst>.

If you would like more information about these materials or about the complete supplements package for *Foundations First*, please contact your local Bedford/St. Martin's sales rep or e-mail <sales_support@bfwpub.com>.

# Contents

**Preface for Instructors** v

**Introduction for Students** xi

**Writing Effective Sentences**

9.1 Identifying Subjects 1
9.2 Recognizing Singular and Plural Subjects 2
9.3 Identifying Subjects and Prepositional Phrases 3
9.4 Identifying Verbs 4
9.5 Identifying Action and Linking Verbs 5
9.6 Identifying Main Verbs and Helping Verbs 6

10.1 Forming Compound Sentences with Coordinating Conjunctions 7
10.2 Forming Compound Sentences with Conjunctive Adverbs 8

11.1 Forming Complex Sentences with Subordinating Conjunctions 10
11.2 Punctuating with Subordinating Conjunctions 11
11.3 Forming Complex Sentences with Subordinating Conjunctions 13
11.4 Choosing the Correct Relative Pronoun 15
11.5 Recognizing Restrictive and Nonrestrictive Clauses 16
11.6 Forming Complex Sentences with Relative Pronouns 17

12.1 Varying Sentence Openings 19
12.2 Choosing Exact Words 20
12.3 Using Concise Language 22

13.1 Recognizing Parallel Structure 23
13.2 Using Parallel Structure 25

**Solving Common Sentence Problems**

14.1 Recognizing Run-ons and Comma Splices 27
14.2 Correcting Run-ons and Comma Splices 28

15.1 Recognizing Sentence Fragments 30
15.2 Correcting Phrase Fragments 31
15.3 Correcting Incomplete Verbs 32
15.4 Correcting Dependent Clause Fragments 33

16.1 Understanding Subject-Verb Agreement 36
16.2 Avoiding Agreement Problems with *Be, Have,* and *Do* 37
16.3 Avoiding Agreement Problems with Compound Subjects 38
16.4 Avoiding Agreement Problems When a Prepositional Phrase Comes between the Subject and the Verb 39
16.5 Avoiding Agreement Problems with Indefinite Nouns as Subjects 40
16.6 Avoiding Agreement Problems When the Verb Comes before the Subject 41
16.7 Avoiding Agreement Problems with *Who, Which,* and *That* 42

17.1 Avoiding Illogical Shifts in Tense 43
17.2 Avoiding Illogical Shifts in Person 44
17.3 Avoiding Illogical Shifts in Voice 45

18.1 Identifying Dangling Modifiers 46
18.2 Correcting Dangling Modifiers 47
18.3 Identifying Misplaced Modifiers 49
18.4 Correcting Misplaced Modifiers 50

**Understanding Basic Grammar**

19.1 Using Regular Verbs in the Past Tense 52
19.2 Using Irregular Verbs in the Past Tense 53
19.3 Using the Past Tense of *Be* 54
19.4 Using the Past Tense of *Can* and *Will* 55

20.1 Using Regular Past Participles 56
20.2 Using Irregular Past Participles 57
20.3 Using the Past and Present Perfect Tenses 58
20.4 Using the Present Perfect and Past Perfect Tenses 59
20.5 Using the Past and Past Perfect Tenses 61
20.6 Using Past Participles as Adjectives 63
20.7 Using Past Participles as Adjectives 64

21.1 Forming Noun Plurals 66

22.1 Identifying Pronoun Antecedents 67
22.2 Understanding Pronoun-Antecedent Agreement 68
22.3 Understanding Pronoun-Antecedent Agreement with Compound Antecedents 69
22.4 Understanding Pronoun-Antecedent Agreement with Indefinite Pronouns 70
22.5 Avoiding Vague Pronouns 71
22.6 Understanding Pronoun Case 73
22.7 Understanding Pronoun Case: Compounds 74
22.8 Understanding Pronoun Case: Comparisons 75
22.9 Understanding Pronoun Case: *Who, Whom* 76
22.10 Understanding Intensive and Reflexive Pronouns 77

23.1 Using Adjectives and Adverbs 78
23.2 Using *Good* and *Well* 79
23.3 Using Comparatives and Superlatives 80
23.4 Using the Comparative and Superlative of *Good/Well* and *Bad/Badly* 82
23.5 Using Demonstrative Adjectives 83

24.1 Avoiding Special Problems with Subjects 84
24.2 Understanding Count and Noncount Nouns 85
24.3 Using Determiners with Count and Noncount Nouns 86
24.4 Understanding Articles 87
24.5 Forming Negative Statements and Questions 88
24.6 Recognizing Stative Verbs 90
24.7 Placing Adjectives in Order 91
24.8 Using Prepositions Correctly 92

**Understanding Punctuation, Mechanics, and Spelling**

25.1 Using Commas in a Series 93
25.2 Using Commas to Set off Introductory Phrases 94
25.3 Using Commas to Set off Parenthetical Words and Phrases 95
25.4 Using Commas with Appositives 96
25.5 Using Commas to Set off Nonrestrictive Clauses 97
25.6 Using Commas in Compound and Complex Sentences 98
25.7 Using Commas in Dates and Addresses 99

26.1 Using Apostrophes to Form Contractions 100
26.2 Using Apostrophes to Form Possessives 101
26.3 Avoiding Special Problems with Apostrophes 102

27.1 Capitalizing Proper Nouns 103
27.2 Punctuating Direct Quotations 104
27.3 Setting off Titles of Works 105

28.1 Deciding between *ie* and *ei* 106
28.2 Understanding Prefixes 107
28.3 Understanding Suffixes 108
28.4 Understanding Suffixes 109

29.1 Spelling Commonly Confused Words 110
29.2 Spelling Commonly Confused Words 111

# *Introduction for Students*

*Supplemental Exercises to Accompany* F*OUNDATIONS* F*IRST* gives you the opportunity to practice the writing skills you are learning in *Foundations First: Sentences and Paragraphs*. Your instructor may assign some of these exercises, or you may decide on your own that you need more practice in a particular area (for example, sentence fragments or subject-verb agreement).

Always begin by reading the section in *Foundations First* that covers the topic you are interested in. (For example, you would read about sentence fragments in Chapter 15.) If, after doing the exercises in that section of *Foundations First*, you want to practice further, turn to the table of contents in *Supplemental Exercises* and find the chapter you are interested in. Keeping *Foundations First* open to that chapter for reference, work through the exercises in *Supplemental Exercises*. Answers to all the exercises appear at the end of the book so that you can check your work as you go along.

Many of the exercises here are also available via Exercise Central, an online exercise collection you can access for free at <bedfordstmartins.com/foundationsfirst>. Exercise Central helps you learn as you go by giving you instant feedback for each item you complete.

Name ______________________________ Section ____________ Date ____________

## ◆ 9.1 Identifying Subjects

For help with this exercise, see section 9A in *Foundations First.* This exercise is also available online (Exercise Central, Chapter 9, 608).

Underline the complete subject of each sentence in the following paragraph. (Be sure to underline not only the noun or pronoun that tells who or what the sentence is about, but also all the words that describe the subject.) Then underline the simple subject once.

*Example:* The Leonid meteor shower happens every November.

(1) Every thirty-three years, the Tempel-Tuttle comet completes its orbit. (2) Nearing the sun, it leaves a trail of dust particles behind. (3) The earth passes through these trails each November. (4) The earth's atmosphere then causes the dust particles to burn up. (5) People on earth see these burning particles, or meteors, as streaks of light in the night sky. (6) The meteors from Tempel-Tuttle's dust appear to come from the constellation Leo. (7) Therefore, the annual November meteor shower is called the Leonid shower. (8) In certain years, such as 2001, our traveling planet passes through several of Tempel-Tuttle's old trails in one evening. (9) On November 18, 2001, some stargazers in North America saw as many as eight hundred meteors an hour during the Leonid shower. (10) Appearing between 4 and 6 a.m. in most parts of the United States, the dazzling display caused many people to lose some sleep.

Name ______________________ Section __________ Date __________

## ◆ 9.2 Recognizing Singular and Plural Subjects

For help with this exercise, see section 9B in *Foundations First.* This exercise is also available online (Exercise Central, Chapter 9, 609).

First, underline the complete subject in each sentence. Then, label each singular subject *S*, and label each plural subject *P*. (Remember that a compound subject is plural.)

*Example:* College students (P) often experience conflict and doubt in their first months at school.

1. A young person may be filled with doubts about going to college.
2. The college years bring about many changes in a person's life.
3. Many freshmen feel anxious about separating from their parents for the first time.
4. Career choices, social situations, relationships, and coursework all require attention from college students.
5. The fear of making bad decisions can paralyze some young people.
6. Depression is becoming fairly common among college students.
7. It can cause students to cut themselves off from other people and fail classes.
8. Many colleges and universities offer counseling services to their students.
9. A therapist can help a student adjust to college life.
10. A manageable level of stress is necessary for a successful college career.

**Name** ______________________________ **Section** __________ **Date** __________

## ◆ 9.3 Identifying Subjects and Prepositional Phrases

For help with this exercise, see section 9C in *Foundations First*. This exercise is also available online (Exercise Central, Chapter 9, 610).

Each of the sentences in the following paragraph includes at least one prepositional phrase. To identify a sentence's subject, first cross out each prepositional phrase. Then, underline the simple subject.

*Example:* Antarctica lies ~~at the bottom of the globe~~.

(1) Emperor penguins live only in Antarctica. (2) Unlike most penguins, emperor penguins lay their eggs during the dark, cold winter months. (3) The female of a penguin pair lays a single egg. (4) Afterward, she goes to sea for two months to find food. (5) Held between the male penguin's feet and his abdomen, the egg remains safe and warm. (6) Male emperor penguins with eggs sleep for twenty hours a day, huddling together for warmth during the incubation period. (7) The males do not eat anything for several weeks. (8) Finally, the chicks hatch in early spring. (9) The mother penguins return to take care of the chicks. (10) Then the hungry fathers travel to the ocean to fatten themselves again.

Name ______________________ Section ____________ Date ____________

## ◆ 9.4 Identifying Verbs

For help with this exercise, see sections 9D and 9E in *Foundations First*. This exercise is also available online (Exercise Central, Chapter 9, 611).

Underline all the action verbs in each of the following sentences.

*Example:* In 1961, Roger Maris hit his sixty-first home run of the season and broke Babe Ruth's 1927 home-run record.

(1) Babe Ruth, one of baseball's most popular players, held the record for home runs in a single season for thirty-four years. (2) In 1961, Roger Maris set a new record over the objections of some fans. (3) Maris, a shy, quiet man, hated attention from reporters and disliked the fame from his home-run record. (4) Nevertheless, Maris's record lasted thirty-seven years. (5) Mark McGwire shattered Maris's record of sixty-one home runs with seventy homers in 1998. (6) Before the end of the 1998 season, McGwire visited the Maris family and won their support. (7) Sportswriters looked again at Maris's accomplishments after McGwire's sixty-second home run that year. (8) Maris's home-run record stayed on the books longer than any other record in baseball. (9) McGwire's record, on the other hand, fell very quickly. (10) In 2001, Barry Bonds outdid McGwire and established a new record of seventy-three home runs in a season.

Name ______________________________ Section __________ Date __________

## ◆ 9.5 Identifying Action and Linking Verbs

For help with this exercise, see sections 9D and 9E in *Foundations First.* This exercise is also available online (Exercise Central, Chapter 9, 612).

Underline the verb in each of the following sentences. Then, in the blank, indicate whether the verb is an action verb (*AV*) or a linking verb (*LV*).

*Example:* During a recession, many companies grow smaller. LV

1. A company with low profits pressures managers to cut costs wherever possible. ______
2. Employees often lose their jobs in a bad economy. ______
3. In hard times, workers feel vulnerable to layoffs and cutbacks. ______
4. As a business policy, a few companies refuse to lay off workers. ______
5. They are eager to economize in other areas. ______
6. Such companies become known for having loyal employees. ______
7. Companies with no-layoff policies seem to many job-seekers to be ideal workplaces. ______
8. However, these companies hire new employees rarely and cautiously. ______
9. They also maintain the smallest possible workforce. ______
10. Job security is difficult to find in both good economies and bad ones. ______

Name ______________________________ Section __________ Date ___________

## ◆ 9.6 Identifying Main Verbs and Helping Verbs

For help with this exercise, see section 9F in *Foundations First.* This exercise is also available online (Exercise Central, Chapter 9, 613).

Some verbs in the following sentences consist of only one word. Others consist of a main verb and one or more helping verbs. In each sentence, underline the complete verb once and the main verb twice.

*Example:* People should keep their domestic cats indoors.

1. Pet cats face many dangers outdoors.
2. Thousands of them are killed by cars every year.
3. Outdoor cats must also deal with other animals and with infectious diseases.
4. In addition, cats can endanger backyard songbirds and small wildlife.
5. There are many good reasons to keep pet cats inside the house.
6. However, they may become obese and bored indoors.
7. For several years, veterinarians have been recommending entertainment for indoor cats.
8. Most cats enjoy the thrill of watching birds through a window or observing fish in an aquarium.
9. Cats can even be trained to do tricks.
10. A caring cat owner will make the cat happy in the house.

Name ______________________________ Section ___________ Date ___________

## ◆ 10.1 Forming Compound Sentences with Coordinating Conjunctions

For help with this exercise, see section 10A in *Foundations First.* This exercise is also available online (Exercise Central, Chapter 10, 614).

Fill in the coordinating conjunction—*and, but, for, nor, or, so,* or *yet*—that most logically links the two parts of each of the following compound sentences. Remember to insert a comma before each coordinating conjunction.

> *Example:* Children need active play __, and__ physical education in school can provide a time and place for it.

(1) Physical education in schools is essential _____ it prepares children to be active and fit adults. (2) Traditional physical education was supposed to interest children in athletic activities _____ too often only those who were already good athletes liked to participate. (3) In traditional physical education classes, students played games well and enjoyed them _____ they played them poorly and disliked them. (4) Children who were not natural athletes often ended up hating physical education _____ many of them never learned to enjoy physical activity, even as adults. (5) Many Americans who do not get any exercise are obese _____ obesity can cause many health problems. (6) Fortunately, a new way of teaching physical education is becoming more common in American schools _____ perhaps children in the future will have a different attitude toward physical activity. (7) The new theory emphasizes fitness rather than athletic skill _____ learning to keep fit benefits more children than learning to play a particular sport. (8) A school gym of the future may contain weight machines, treadmills, and in-line skates _____ children can participate in activities like the ones adults do at health clubs. (9) The students will not be graded on how well they can play a sport _____ they will be expected to work hard enough to keep their heart rate at a target level. (10) This physical education plan would appeal to most educators _____ many parents would also see the plan as a great improvement over the physical education classes of the past.

Name ______________________ Section __________ Date __________

## ◆ 10.2 Forming Compound Sentences with Conjunctive Adverbs

For help with this exercise, see section 10C in *Foundations First.* This exercise is also available online (Exercise Central, Chapter 10, 615).

Consulting the list of conjunctive adverbs on page 000 and the list of transitional expressions on page 000, choose a word or expression that logically connects each pair of sentences into one compound sentence. Be sure to punctuate appropriately.

> *Example:* Accidents kill thousands of drivers and passengers in cars every year; however, the ~~The~~ proper use of seat belts saves countless lives.

1. Laws in most states require people in the front seats of cars to wear seat belts. Only a few states make rear-seat passengers wear safety belts.

2. Rear-seat passengers who do not put on their seat belts can be seriously injured in an accident. They can hurt people in the front seat.

3. In some states, people who were not wearing seat belts collect reduced damages if they are hurt in an accident. They must bear some of the financial responsibility for their injury.

4. Any unrestrained person, animal, or thing in a car can be dangerous in an accident. Car owners should look closely at everything they carry in the car.

5. Storing loose objects in the trunk of the car is the best way to avoid danger. Putting a bag of groceries in the trunk prevents a can of soup from flying at a person's head after a sudden stop.

6. Many SUVs and station wagons do not have trunks for storing luggage, groceries, and other items. Such vehicles have a storage space behind the passenger seats.

7. Unrestrained objects can become projectiles and kill someone. Car-safety specialists recommend cargo dividers or nets to prevent injury from objects in the backs of SUVs and station wagons.

8. All states require young children to be buckled into a special car seat. Injuries to young children in car accidents are less common than they were a decade ago.

9. The law allows pets to roam freely in the car. Animals can also suffer injuries or hurt someone else in an accident.

10. Wearing a seat belt is sensible. Not only front-seat passengers, but all people, animals, and objects are safer in a car when they are restrained.

Name ______________________________ Section __________ Date __________

## ◆ 11.1 Forming Complex Sentences with Subordinating Conjunctions

For help with this exercise, see section 11A in *Foundations First*. This exercise is also available online (Exercise Central, Chapter 11, 616).

Write an appropriate subordinating conjunction in each blank. Consult the list of subordinating conjunctions on page 000 to make sure you choose a conjunction that establishes the proper relationship between ideas. (The required punctuation has been provided.)

*Example:* ___When___ Garth Fagan began his dance career, he was still in his teens.

(1) __________ he won a Tony Award for choreography for his work on the Broadway show *The Lion King*, Garth Fagan's name has been well known. (2) The choreographer began as a dancer with a dance company in Jamaica, __________ he was born. (3) As a young man, Fagan first studied with Ivy Baxter and other Caribbean dance teachers and performers __________ he moved to New York City to work with modern dancers like Martha Graham and Alvin Ailey. (4) __________ he graduated from college in 1969, Fagan lived briefly in Detroit and then moved to Rochester, New York, to found his own dance company. (5) Fagan then stopped dancing __________ he could devote his attention to choreography and to instructing the fourteen members of the company, Garth Fagan Dance. (6) Fagan chose untrained dancers for his troupe __________ he felt that he could more easily teach them his unique style of movement. (7) __________ Fagan's choreography is one of a kind, he acknowledges sources including modern dance, traditional Afro-Caribbean dance, and ballet. (8) His African-inspired dances for *The Lion King* were seen by many more audiences __________ Fagan could attract in the relatively small world of dance performances. (9) In addition to his enormous Broadway success, Fagan has continued to win prestigious prizes __________ he goes. (10) __________ his dancers can share his success, he uses prize money to pay them good wages and offer them medical benefits.

Name ______________________________ Section __________ Date __________

## ◆ 11.2 Punctuating with Subordinating Conjunctions

For help with this exercise, see section 11B in *Foundations First*. This exercise is also available online (Exercise Central, Chapter 11, 617).

Some of the following complex sentences are punctuated correctly, and some are not. Put a *C* next to every sentence that is correctly punctuated. If the punctuation is not correct, edit the sentence to correct it.

*Example:* Although ice and snow are common during the winter months in Quebec City, a million visitors attend the winter carnival there every year. __C__

1. Many people travel to winter carnivals in Rio de Janeiro and New Orleans, because the parties are famously wild and the weather is warm in those cities. ______

2. Whereas visitors to Rio and New Orleans are often seeking escape from the cold the attractions at Quebec City's winter carnival emphasize ice and snow. ______

3. Since Canadian winters can be long and harsh, the Carneval de Quebec has been held for more than a century to give the citizens something to do in mid-winter. ______

4. Although canoes are no longer essential for transportation in Quebec the Carneval de Quebec honors tradition with canoe races across the St. Lawrence River. ______

5. Sculptors come from all over the world, so that they can compete in the ice-sculpting and snow-sculpting competitions held every year during the Carneval de Quebec. ______

6. If people attending the carnival are not awed by the snow and ice sculptures, they may be awed by the fact that some of the snow-sculpting teams that compete are from warm countries such as Mexico. ______

7. Carnival visitors gasp, as they stare at a palace made of seven hundred tons of ice. ______

8. After the sky grows dark each evening, fireworks light up the ice palace. ______

9. Alcohol was served during most events at the Carneval de Quebec until city officials decided to make the festival more child-friendly in 1995. ______

10. Even though cognac breakfasts are no longer part of the winter carnival children and grown-ups alike can still get a thrill from inner-tube sledding. ______

Name ______________________ Section __________ Date __________

## ◆ 11.3 Forming Complex Sentences with Subordinating Conjunctions

For help with this exercise, see sections 11A and 11B in *Foundations First.* This exercise is also available online (Exercise Central, Chapter 11, 618).

Use the subordinating conjunction in parentheses to combine each sentence pair. Make sure you include a comma where one is required.

*Example:* ~~A~~ If a child decides to become a vegetarian, ~~Parents~~ parents have to make important decisions about family meals. (if)

1. Parents should try to keep families together at mealtimes. Individual family members have an opportunity to talk and spend time together. (so that)

2. Getting a family to eat meals together is a challenge in modern America. The only problem is scheduling. (even if)

3. Someone in the family requires a special diet. The challenge of figuring out how to eat together becomes even more difficult. (once)

4. Some children discover where their meat comes from. They no longer want to eat meat. (when)

5. Being a vegetarian may be a lifelong choice. It may also be a phase a child is going through. (although)

6. The parent who prepares meals is not used to vegetarian cooking. A child's decision not to eat meat can cause conflicts. (if)

7. A vegetarian diet can be even healthier than a diet containing meat. Other family members may not be vegetarians. (while)

8. Some parents prefer to begin cooking vegetarian meals for the whole family. A child wants to eat meatless meals. (while)

9. Other parents prepare two different meals for the family. The children who will not eat meat are unable to cook their own preferred foods. (provided)

10. Food should unite families instead of dividing them. Psychologists say that whenever possible, parents should not overreact by forcing children to eat food that they dislike. (because)

Name ______________________ Section __________ Date __________

## ◆ 11.4 Choosing the Correct Relative Pronoun

For help with this exercise, see section 11C in *Foundations First.* This exercise is also available online (Exercise Central, Chapter 11, 619).

In each of the following complex sentences, underline the dependent clause once and underline the relative pronoun twice. Then draw an arrow from the relative pronoun to the noun or pronoun it describes.

*Example:* Benjamin Franklin, who mastered many trades, was one of the signers of the Declaration of Independence.

1. The education that Benjamin Franklin received in Boston schools ended when he was ten.
2. His older brother James, who ran a print shop, took Benjamin on as an apprentice.
3. Although he never returned to school, Franklin read every book that he could find.
4. He studied the British journal *The Spectator*, which taught him to write clearly and effectively.
5. After he quarreled with the brother who had given him the apprenticeship, Benjamin Franklin left Boston for Philadelphia.
6. Franklin's formula for business success, which served him well as a printer and newspaper publisher, was to work harder than his competition.
7. Franklin was also a pioneering scientist who conducted experiments with electricity.
8. Inventions that he created include bifocals and wood-burning stoves.
9. Franklin was the only person to sign all four of the documents that ended the original colonies' ties with Great Britain and created the United States.
10. At the end of his life, Franklin served as president of America's first antislavery society, which asked the U.S. Congress to abolish slavery.

Name ______________________ Section __________ Date __________

## ◆ 11.5 Recognizing Restrictive and Nonrestrictive Clauses

For help with this exercise, see section 11D in *Foundations First.* This exercise is also available online (Exercise Central, Chapter 11, 620).

Read the following sentences. If the dependent clause in the sentence is restrictive, write *R* in the blank; if the clause is nonrestrictive, write *N*. Then, if necessary, correct the punctuation of the sentence.

*Example:* People/ who were diagnosed with ulcers/ were once told that rest and relaxation would cure the problem. __R__

1. For many years, ulcers which are irritated places on the stomach lining have been attributed to stress. ______
2. In 1982, physicians who had been studying ulcers, discovered a different cause. ______
3. Surprisingly, most ulcers are caused by a common bacterium, that is called *H. pylori*. ______
4. Patients whose symptoms were caused by *H. pylori* could be cured with antibiotics. ______
5. However, stress which has bad effects on health in other ways may still have some responsibility for ulcers. ______
6. Ulcers do not always strike people, who have *H. pylori* in their systems. ______
7. What is the trigger that causes the bacterium to create an ulcer? ______
8. According to some scientists, stress may create conditions, that allow *H. pylori* to cause an ulcer. ______
9. Former prisoners of war who have often suffered enough stress to be traumatized are more likely to develop ulcers. ______
10. A person's mental state, which may be positive or negative, can have an effect on health. ______

Name ______________________ Section __________ Date __________

## ◆ 11.6 Forming Complex Sentences with Relative Pronouns

For help with this exercise, see sections 11C and 11D in *Foundations First.* This exercise is also available online (Exercise Central, Chapter 11, 621).

Combine each of the following pairs of sentences into one complex sentence, using the relative pronoun that follows the pair. Be sure to punctuate correctly, using commas to set off only nonrestrictive clauses, not restrictive clauses.

*Example:* Many people ^who study environmental conditions around the world/ ~~They~~ see water shortages as the most severe problem facing the earth in the next century. (who)

1. Problems come with an increasing world population. They include finding enough food for growing numbers of people. (that)

2. People around the globe rely on farmland for their food. Farmland has become increasingly productive in the past century. (which)

3. A small farm might have fed a single family in 1900. Today, a small farm can produce more and better crops, thanks to fertilizers, pest controls, and other innovations. (that)

4. Farmers grow the crops to feed people all over the world. They need water to have a successful harvest. (who)

5. Scientists study climate. Most of these scientists believe global warming is a reality. (who)

6. Global warming may cause only slight increases in world temperatures in the next century. It can still disrupt rainfall patterns greatly. (which)

7. People live in the Great Plains. They get much of their water from underground aquifers in that dry part of the United States. (who)

8. As less rain falls, people use more water from the aquifers. The aquifers will dry out in just a few decades at this rate of use. (which)

9. Other countries face even more severe water shortages than the United States. These countries have fast-growing populations and shrinking supplies of water. (that)

10. A group of national leaders has met to discuss the world's water problem. The problem is likely to get worse before it gets better. (which)

Name ______________________ Section __________ Date __________

## ◆ 12.1 Varying Sentence Openings

For help with this exercise, see section 12A in *Foundations First.* This exercise is also available online (Exercise Central, Chapter 12, 622).

Several sentences in the following passage contain adverbs and prepositional phrases that could be moved to the beginnings of the sentences. Revise the passage to vary the sentence openings by moving adverbs to the beginnings of three sentences and moving prepositional phrases to the beginnings of three other sentences. Be sure to place a comma after these adverbs and prepositional phrases.

*Example:* In the consumer electronics industry, buyers ~~Buyers~~ often think they are getting bargains ~~in the consumer electronics industry~~.

(1) Manufacturers usually suggest a retail price that their products should carry. (2) Retailers may, however, set any price that they like. (3) Sellers in the consumer electronics field are very likely to set prices lower than the manufacturers suggest. (4) Store prices are often two or three hundred dollars lower than the manufacturer's suggested retail price for items like digital cameras and big-screen televisions. (5) Consumers were asked in a recent study whether they had paid full price for their latest electronics purchase. (6) Seventy-five percent of the participants, surprisingly, claimed to have gotten their merchandise on sale. (7) Researchers wondered afterward whether the terms *list price* and *sale price* have any meaning when so many people buy products "on sale." (8) Manufacturers indeed seem to set their list prices artificially high. (9) They can allow sellers to claim that their prices are twenty or forty percent lower than list price by doing this. (10) Consumers may not be hurt in the end by the fact that so-called list prices are usually fictional, but the practice is not precisely honest.

Name ______________________ Section ____________ Date ____________

## ◆ 12.2 Choosing Exact Words

For help with this exercise, see section 12B in *Foundations First.* This exercise is also available online (Exercise Central, Chapter 12, 623).

Here are ten general words. In the blank beside each, write a more specific word related to the general word. Then, use the more specific word in a sentence of your own.

*Example:* animal black and white kitten

The black and white kitten sat on the doorstep, purring with great satisfaction.

1. entertainment ______________________

2. store ______________________

3. move ______________________

4. child ______________________

5. picture ______________________

6. transportation ______________________________

______________________________________________________________________

______________________________________________________________________

7. nice ______________________________

______________________________________________________________________

______________________________________________________________________

8. house ______________________________

______________________________________________________________________

______________________________________________________________________

9. work ______________________________

______________________________________________________________________

______________________________________________________________________

10. feel ______________________________

______________________________________________________________________

______________________________________________________________________

Name ______________________ Section __________ Date __________

## ◆ 12.3 Using Concise Language

For help with this exercise, see section 12C in *Foundations First.* This exercise is also available online (Exercise Central, Chapter 12, 624).

To make the following sentences more concise, cross out wordy expressions and unnecessary repetition, substituting more concise expressions where necessary.

*Example:* ~~It is a fact that silent~~ Silent films are gaining popularity again.

1. In 1893, Thomas Edison set up the original first movie studio.
2. The first films were silent due to the fact that the technology for movies with sound did not exist.
3. Early silent movies looked jumpy and jerky.
4. The first silent films were also short in length, but studios later made full-length silents.
5. At the present time, film scholars acknowledge that some silents were masterpieces.
6. When the possibility of making movies with sound became possible, the silents were doomed.
7. There was an Al Jolson film in 1927 called *The Jazz Singer* that was the first "talkie."
8. Despite the fact that silent movies were still popular, film studios decided that talking pictures and silent pictures could not both please moviegoers.
9. Some studios released silent movies that played too fast at the wrong speed to prevent audiences from enjoying them.
10. The global popularity around the world of silent films on television and at film festivals proves that the best silents can still attract audiences.

Name ______________________ Section __________ Date __________

## ◆ 13.1 Recognizing Parallel Structure

For help with this exercise, see section 13A in *Foundations First.* This exercise is also available online (Exercise Central, Chapter 13, 625).

In each of the following sentences, decide whether or not the underlined words are parallel. If they are, write *P* in the blank. If they are not, edit the sentence to make the words parallel.

*Examples*: Some people like sandwiches best on bread that is soft, white, and spongy. P

Can a dish that contains bright red gelatin, fruit, and ~~has~~ mayonnaise ~~in it~~ really be considered a salad? ______

1. The traditional foods of a culture remind people of their shared past and are a way to bind them together in the future. ______

2. The foods of immigrants sometimes become part of the majority culture; Italian food and eating Chinese dishes have become popular all over the United States. ______

3. A former empire may adopt food brought back from its colonies, as the Dutch love Indonesian restaurants and the British adore Indian ones. ______

4. Sometimes, however, one culture's favorite foods leave people from other cultures uninterested or they even feel disgusted. ______

5. For example, Marmite, a brown, salty, yeast-based spread, is a delicacy in England. ______

6. Even Marmite's makers admit that the pungent odor of Marmite and its tasting extremely strong offend some people. ______

7. Around the world, foods like fermented eggs and insect larvae attract faithful devotees, passionate opponents, and very few diners are indifferent to them. ______

8. Regional foods in the United States are treasured in one area and people have never heard of them elsewhere. ______

9. New Yorkers eat knishes, Louisianans consume boudin, and Coloradans sample Rocky Mountain oysters. ______

10. When people try to communicate across cultures, it is often easier at first to get to know others through their food than appreciating different social customs. ______

Name ________________ Section ________ Date ________

## ◆ 13.2 Using Parallel Structure

For help with this exercise, see section 13B in *Foundations First.* This exercise is also available online (Exercise Central, Chapter 13, 626).

Rewrite the following sentences to achieve parallel structure.

*Example:* The Miss America pageant has been both a straightforward beauty pageant and it has been a scholarship program.

The Miss America pageant has been both a straightforward beauty pageant and a scholarship program.

1. The first beauty pageants in the United States featured women wearing bathing suits and they posed at the seaside.

______________________________

______________________________

2. In the 1920s, many Americans felt that women who put themselves on display in a beauty contest were not moral, decent, and could not be respected.

______________________________

______________________________

3. Many young women who participated in early Miss America contests wanted either to win a Hollywood film contract or they hoped for a career on the stage.

______________________________

______________________________

4. Lenora Slaughter, who was hired by Miss America pageant promoters in 1935, added a talent competition, persuaded society women to act as chaperones for the contestants, and she convinced sponsors to offer the winners college scholarships.

______________________________

______________________________

5. Bess Myerson, Miss America 1945, was not only the first scholarship winner but also she was the first Jewish Miss America.

______________________________

______________________________

6. In the 1930s, pageant rules required contestants to be young, single, and they had to be white.

7. Until the 1970s, neither the pageant's finalists nor were any of the contestants African American or Latina.

8. Vanessa Williams's victory in 1983 was historic both because she was the first African-American winner and no previous winner had to resign after a scandal.

9. Williams may be the best-known Miss America, but she has made her name more as an actress and singer than by being the winner of the Miss America pageant.

10. Pageant promoters emphasize that Miss America must have brains and be talented, but even brilliant contestants will not advance very far if they have extra pounds or unconventional looks.

Name ______________________ Section __________ Date __________

## ◆ 14.1 Recognizing Run-ons and Comma Splices

For help with this exercise, see section 14A in *Foundations First.* This exercise is also available online (Exercise Central, Chapter 14, 627).

Some of the sentences in the following passage are correct, but others are run-ons or comma splices. In the blank after each sentence, write *C* if the sentence is correct, *RO* if it is a run-on, and *CS* if it is a comma splice.

*Example:* Puppies are adorable they require a lot of attention and care. RO

(1) We decided to get a dog last year, my sister wanted to get a puppy. ______ (2) My mother insisted on an adult dog she wanted to save an animal from a shelter. ______ (3) We adopted a seven-year-old dog from the local Humane Society. ______ (4) The Humane Society officials were pleased few people want to adopt older dogs. ______ (5) Everyone at the Humane Society wished us well, they gave us tips on training our new pet. ______ (6) Fortunately, our dog was already housebroken that made owning him much easier. ______ (7) He did have some bad habits, such as jumping on visitors. ______ (8) We signed him up for classes with a local dog trainer, the trainer helped us teach him better manners. ______ (9) Now our dog has been a part of the family for several months, we can hardly imagine life without him. ______ (10) A puppy might have been cuter however, this dog has a winning personality. ______

Name ______________________________ Section ____________ Date ____________

## ◆ 14.2 Correcting Run-ons and Comma Splices

For help with this exercise, see section 14B in *Foundations First.* This exercise is also available online (Exercise Central, Chapter 14, 628).

Correct the run-ons and comma splices in the following sentences in one of five ways: create two separate sentences; connect ideas with a comma and a coordinating conjunction; connect ideas with a semicolon; connect ideas with a semicolon and a conjunctive adverb or transitional expression; or connect ideas with a subordinating conjunction or relative pronoun.

*Example:* The Super Bowl ^, which^ takes place in midwinter every year ^,^ ~~it~~ is traditionally one of the most-watched shows on television.

1. The end of the football season in the United States is marked by the Super Bowl, it is the championship game between the winner of the American Football Conference and the winner of the National Football Conference.

2. No football fan misses the big game many people with little interest in football also turn on their televisions.

3. The Super Bowl is famous for its advertisements many advertisers introduce new campaigns during the game.

4. Advertisers pay top dollar for Super Bowl ad time, they know that an enormous audience for their advertisements is guaranteed.

5. The Super Bowl often has higher ratings than any other television show of the year, even the shows that come on after the game attract record numbers of viewers.

6. Super Bowl advertisements are often some of the best things on television they may have cutting-edge technology or naughty humor.

7. Many Americans have a Super Bowl tradition, fans gather at someone's home to spend the afternoon eating, drinking, and watching the game.

8. People attending a Super Bowl party expect certain kinds of food, newspapers print Super Bowl party recipes for weeks before the game.

9. Super Sunday promotions bombard Americans throughout the month of January, retailers offer specials on any item that can be linked to football.

10. Baseball is supposed to be America's national pastime people witnessing Super Bowl hysteria must imagine that football is at least as popular.

Name ______________________________ Section __________ Date ___________

## ◆ 15.1 Recognizing Sentence Fragments

For help with this exercise, see section 15A in *Foundations First*. This exercise is also available online (Exercise Central, Chapter 15, 629).

In the following passage, some of the numbered groups of words are missing a subject, a verb, or both. First, identify each fragment by labeling it *F*. Next, decide how each fragment could be attached to a nearby word group to create a complete new sentence. Finally, rewrite the entire passage, using complete sentences, on the lines provided.

*Example:* Japanese animated films have a history. _____ That goes back to the 1960s. __F__

Japanese animated films have a history that goes back to the 1960s.

(1) The man behind Japanese animation was an illustrator. _____ (2) Named Osamu Tezuka. _____ (3) He admired Disney animation. _____ (4) And created a comic book in 1951 about a robot child. _____ (5) After the success of the comic book. _____ (6) Tezuka turned it into an animated television show called *Astro Boy*. _____ (7) It attracted viewers all over the world. _____ (8) Japanese animated films and television programs are still hugely popular. _____ (9) With audiences in Japan. _____ (10) And are loved by growing numbers of people in America. _____

Name ________________ Section ________ Date ________

## ◆ 15.2 Correcting Phrase Fragments

For help with this exercise, see section 15B in *Foundations First*. This exercise is also available online (Exercise Central, Chapter 15, 630).

In the following passage, some of the numbered groups of words are appositive fragments or prepositional phrase fragments. First, underline each fragment. Then, decide how each fragment could be attached to a nearby word group to create a complete new sentence. Finally, rewrite the entire passage, using complete sentences, on the lines provided.

*Example:* For many years. China had a terrible environmental record.

For many years, China had a terrible environmental record.

(1) Economic growth has been more important than clean air and water. (2) In China for decades. (3) Under the Kyoto Protocol. (4) An agreement among industrialized and developing nations to decrease pollution and limit global warming. (5) China will have to reduce carbon emissions from factories and cars. (6) Many supporters of the Kyoto agreement feared that China would resist changes. (7) In the nation's environmental policy. (8) According to Xie Zhenhua. (9) The director of China's State Environmental Protection Administration. (10) The Kyoto agreement will, in fact, benefit both the global environment and China's economy.

Name ______________________ Section __________ Date __________

## ◆ 15.3 Correcting Incomplete Verbs

For help with this exercise, see section 15C in *Foundations First*. This exercise is also available online (Exercise Central, Chapter 15, 631).

Each of the following is a fragment because it does not have a complete verb. Correct each fragment by completing the verb.

*Example:* Olive ^was born in October 2004.

1. Melissa expecting her first child last fall.
2. She and her husband Julio been married now for twelve years.
3. Before their wedding, they chosen not to have a baby right away.
4. After five years of marriage, they planning for a child.
5. Melissa's mother been hoping for a grandchild since the wedding.
6. Julio's parents not getting any younger, either.
7. The pressure making them very unhappy because they really wanted a baby.
8. At last, in the spring of 2004, Melissa and Julio learned that they going to have a daughter.
9. They never known such happiness before that day.
10. Their baby girl being treated like a princess by her parents and grandparents.

Name ____________________ Section __________ Date __________

## ◆ 15.4 Correcting Dependent Clause Fragments

For help with this exercise, see section 15D in *Foundations First*. This exercise is also available online (Exercise Central, Chapter 15, 632).

Correct each of the following dependent clause fragments in two ways. First, make the fragment a complete sentence by adding a group of words that completes the idea. Second, make the fragment a complete sentence by deleting the subordinating conjunction or relative pronoun that makes the idea incomplete.

*Example:* The actor who politely accepted the award.

REVISED:

The actor who politely accepted the award starred in my favorite movie.

REVISED:

The actor politely accepted the award.

1. When the car skidded across the intersection.

REVISED:

____________________

____________________

REVISED:

____________________

____________________

2. A package that had been left on the floor of the post office.

REVISED:

____________________

____________________

REVISED:

____________________

____________________

3. Because my mother won't allow it.

REVISED:

REVISED:

4. The woman who hired his new boss.

REVISED:

REVISED:

5. Before we realized what was happening.

REVISED:

REVISED:

6. My brother, who works for a catering company.

REVISED:

REVISED:

7. Although city officials refuse to discuss the power plant.

REVISED:

REVISED:

8. While the moon was full.

REVISED:

REVISED:

9. The proposal, which will certainly be approved this month.

REVISED:

REVISED:

10. The speech that the president made.

REVISED:

REVISED:

Name ______________________________ Section ____________ Date ____________

## ◆ 16.1 Understanding Subject-Verb Agreement

For help with this exercise, see section 16A in *Foundations First*. This exercise is also available online (Exercise Central, Chapter 16, 633).

Fill in the blank with the correct present tense form of the verb in parentheses.

*Example:* Business executives ____write____ (write) many memos and e-mails at work.

(1) A new study ______________ (show) some interesting facts about the mistakes business writers make. (2) The researchers learned that the best-paid executives ______________ (tend) to be the sloppiest writers. (3) Their e-mails ______________ (contain) more spelling and grammar errors than other workers' communications do. (4) Perhaps an executive ______________ (want) to show that he or she is too busy and important to proofread. (5) Perhaps corporate chiefs ______________ (expect) their assistants to make any necessary changes. (6) On the other hand, middle managers ______________ (use) the most jargon. (7) Apparently, the average middle manager ______________ (feel) that longer, wordier messages can attract attention. (8) By writing such messages, a mid-level executive ______________ (hope) to move up to the next level. (9) Then, presumably, he or she ______________ (start) to misspell words and make grammatical errors like the big bosses do. But students taking business courses should not neglect their English classes just yet. (10) In order to get hired in corporate America in the first place, job applicants ______________ (need) good writing skills.

Name ______________________ Section ____________ Date ____________

## ◆ 16.2 Avoiding Agreement Problems with *Be, Have,* and *Do*

For help with this exercise, see section 16B in *Foundations First*. This exercise is also available online (Exercise Central, Chapter 16, 634).

Fill in the blank with the correct present tense form of the verb in parentheses.

*Example:* Many teenagers ___are___ (be) likely to communicate with instant messaging software.

1. Many young people today ____________ (have) computers in their homes.
2. A modern high school student ____________ (do) a lot of homework on a computer.
3. Instant messaging ____________ (be) a new way to converse with friends online.
4. An instant message ____________ (have) an immediate audience.
5. However, the message writers ____________ (have) some privacy because they can neither see nor hear each other.
6. Many people ____________ (do) other tasks while they are sending and receiving instant messages.
7. I ____________ (be) a big fan of instant messaging.
8. Sometimes several friends ____________ (be) online at the same time, so we can have a conversation.
9. My parents ____________ (have) questions about the value of instant messaging over telephoning or seeing people personally.
10. I tell them that we ____________ (do) our share of talking on the telephone and in person, too.

Name ______________________ Section __________ Date __________

## ◆ 16.3 Avoiding Agreement Problems with Compound Subjects

For help with this exercise, see section 16C in *Foundations First*. This exercise is also available online (Exercise Central, Chapter 16, 635).

Underline the correct verb in each of the following sentences.

*Example:* My sister and her fiancé (wants, want) to be marine biologists.

1. My sister Nicole and her fiancé Phil (visits, visit) southern Florida frequently.
2. Usually, Nicole or he (suggests, suggest) snorkeling in the coral reefs there.
3. Coral and sponges (lives, live) in the tropical ocean water.
4. Plants and marine animals (is, are) important parts of an underwater ecosystem.
5. Manatees or other sea creatures (swims, swim) quite close to Nicole and Phil on most of their snorkeling trips.
6. Boat motors and polluted water (is, are) dangerous to manatees, the gentle marine mammals.
7. Scars or even an injured limb (marks, mark) many a manatee after a collision with a boat's motor.
8. Florida panthers and key deer (dies, die) too often on highways in the Florida Keys.
9. Florida panthers and manatees (remains, remain) on the list of endangered species.
10. Florida's wildlife or tourism (is, are) bound to suffer, for both cannot be protected at the same time.

Name ______________________ Section __________ Date __________

## ◆ 16.4 Avoiding Agreement Problems When a Prepositional Phrase Comes between the Subject and the Verb

For help with this exercise, see section 16D in *Foundations First*. This exercise is also available online (Exercise Central, Chapter 16, 636).

In each of the following sentences, cross out the prepositional phrase that separates the subject and the verb. Then underline the simple subject of the sentence once and the verb that agrees with the subject twice.

*Example:* The island ~~of Manhattan~~ (lies, lie) between the East River and the Hudson River.

1. The skyline of New York (appears, appear) in many movies.
2. The Empire State Building on Thirty-Fourth Street (remains, remain) a landmark.
3. The twin towers of the World Trade Center (stands, stand) no longer at the foot of Manhattan.
4. Residents of the area (misses, miss) the familiar sight.
5. A controversy over depictions of the twin towers (exists, exist) among some filmmakers.
6. Movies in the city and elsewhere (is, are) filmed long before their release to the public.
7. A film with New York settings (is, are) often likely to contain footage of the missing towers.
8. Many of the directors (wants, want) to remove the World Trade Center from their films.
9. The sight of the World Trade Center (seems, seem) certain to distract moviegoers.
10. However, New York views with the empty skyline (calls, call) attention to the towers' absence.

Name ______________________ Section __________ Date __________

## ◆ 16.5 Avoiding Agreement Problems with Indefinite Nouns as Subjects

For help with this exercise, see section 16E in *Foundations First*. This exercise is also available online (Exercise Central, Chapter 16, 637).

Underline the correct verb in each of the following sentences.

*Example:* Of all the parents I know, few (remembers, <u>remember</u>) a time before *Sesame Street*.

(1) Around the United States, almost everyone under five (watches, watch) *Sesame Street* on public television. (2) Neither of my sons (wants, want) to miss a single episode. (3) Everybody on the show (seems, seem) like an old friend. (4) On most episodes, someone (speaks, speak) Spanish, so my boys are hearing two languages when they watch. (5) Nothing (makes, make) learning a foreign language easier than hearing one in childhood, so I know this will help them later in life. (6) In the twenty-first century, one of the tasks facing *Sesame Street* (is, are) dealing with other cultures. (7) No one (expects, expect) the show to stop teaching children their letters and numbers. (8) On new shows, however, someone (is, are) likely to talk about world religions or other beliefs. (9) Among other countries in the world, many (offers, offer) the children's program in the local language. (10) With so many cultures paying attention to *Sesame Street*, each (has, have) an opportunity to teach children tolerance of differences.

Name ______________________ Section __________ Date __________

## ◆ 16.6 Avoiding Agreement Problems When the Verb Comes before the Subject

For help with this exercise, see section 16F in *Foundations First*. This exercise is also available online (Exercise Central, Chapter 16, 638).

Underline the simple subject of each sentence. Then circle the correct form of the verb.

*Example:* What (is, are) Asperger's syndrome?

1. There (is, are) more boys than girls with Asperger's syndrome.
2. What (is, are) the symptoms of this condition?
3. There (is, are) often an obsession with some subject.
4. There (was, were) a boy in my kindergarten class fascinated by U.S. presidents.
5. There (was, were) few other five-year-olds with such interests.
6. There (has, have) been children obsessed with religion, too.
7. How (does, do) parents cope with this syndrome?
8. There (is, are) agreement among experts about the benefits of therapy.
9. What (is, are) the prospects for a child with Asperger's syndrome?
10. There (is, are) hope for a relatively normal life.

Name ______________________ Section __________ Date __________

## ◆ 16.7 Avoiding Agreement Problems with *Who, Which,* and *That*

For help with this exercise, see section 16G in *Foundations First*. This exercise is also available online (Exercise Central, Chapter 16, 000).

In the blank, write the word that *who, which,* or *that* refers to. Then underline the correct form of the verb.

*Example:* Grand Canyon The Grand Canyon, which (was, were) one of the first U.S. national parks, is severely overcrowded.

__________ 1. Summer visitors who (comes, come) to Grand Canyon National Park may be surprised by their experience.

__________ 2. The Mather Point overlook, which (offers, offer) wonderful views of the canyon, can provide only sixty-five parking spaces.

__________ 3. On a summer day, more than a thousand cars that (arrives, arrive) at Mather Point must compete for those spaces.

__________ 4. Tourists who (expects, expect) a serene view often get into fist-fights.

__________ 5. The canyon's highways are not immune from the road rage that (is, are) found in other parts of the country.

__________ 6. The people who (drives, drive) over 6,000 cars to the Grand Canyon on an average summer day must hope to win one of the 2,400 parking spaces available.

__________ 7. Overcrowding is a problem that (has, have) concerned Park Service planners for over a decade.

__________ 8. A light railway that (was, were) supposed to limit the use of private cars inside the national park may not be built after all.

__________ 9. The park's budget, which (comes, come) from the federal government, ran into opponents in Congress.

__________ 10. So far, no trains or tracks go to the Grand Canyon train station, which (was, were) completed in 2000.

Name ______________________ Section __________ Date __________

## ◆ 17.1 Avoiding Illogical Shifts in Tense

For help with this exercise, see section 17A in *Foundations First*. This exercise is also available online (Exercise Central, Chapter 17, 639).

Edit the following sentences for illogical shifts in tense. If a sentence is correct, write *C* in the blank.

*Example:* By 1946, Langston Hughes was a famous writer, and the photographer Henri Cartier Bresson ~~takes~~ took his picture.

_____

(1) Langston Hughes remains one of the twentieth century's best-known poets, a man famous enough to be featured on a U.S. postage stamp. _____ (2) Hughes was born in Missouri and spends his first twelve years in Kansas. _____ (3) Although he was now associated with the Harlem Renaissance of the 1920s, he did not arrive in New York until 1921. _____ (4) At the time, he is nineteen years old. _____ (5) Hughes quickly makes a name for himself with his poetry, publishing "The Negro Speaks of Rivers" in a national magazine that same year. _____ (6) Because he wanted only to write, not to teach or to work in an office, Hughes tries nearly every kind of writing. _____ (7) He published short stories, a play, essays, and a novel, and he also wrote newspaper columns and children's books._____ (8) During his life, his poetry was very popular, and it was still widely read today. _____ (9) A line from "The Negro Speaks of Rivers" adorns the floor of the Langston Hughes Auditorium, which stands in Harlem. _____ (10) Blue stone in the shape of a river decorates the floor of the auditorium, and an urn containing Hughes's ashes rested underneath the stone. _____

Name ____________________ Section __________ Date __________

## ◆ 17.2 Avoiding Illogical Shifts in Person

For help with this exercise, see section 17B in *Foundations First*. This exercise is also available online (Exercise Central, Chapter 17, 640).

The following paragraph contains illogical shifts in person. Edit it so that pronouns are used consistently. Be sure to change the verb if necessary to make it agree with the new subject.

*Example:* My friend Sara has a difficult boss, and ~~you~~ she never ~~know~~ knows what problems she will have at work.

(1) My friend Sara works at a local historic house where you can take tours. (2) Sara tells you terrible stories about her boss. (3) The boss yells whenever you alter a single word of the speech that the visitors hear. (4) Sara has won prizes at some of the public-speaking contests you can enter at school. (5) She tries occasionally to give the visitors information about the house that you wouldn't ordinarily hear. (6) However, the boss is only happy when you recite the memorized speech word for word. (7) Recently, Sara was giving a tour to a group, and you could see that the mayor was one of the visitors. (8) She told the group some things that you learn by working at the house—things that are not part of the speech. (9) Her boss overheard, and you thought he was going to explode. (10) Afterward, however, the mayor told Sara that you can apply to work as a summer assistant in the mayor's office and that she would be sure to remember Sara's name.

Name ______________________________ Section __________ Date __________

## ◆ 17.3 Avoiding Illogical Shifts in Voice

For help with this exercise, see section 17C in *Foundations First*. This exercise is also available online (Exercise Central, Chapter 17, 642).

Correct any illogical shifts in voice in the following sentences, using active voice wherever possible. If necessary, change any verbs that do not agree with the new subjects. If a sentence is correct, write *C* in the blank.

*Example:* The parrot squawked at the little girl, and ^she answered the bird ~~was answered by her~~ with a whistle.

1. Martin drove his car too fast, and a speeding ticket was received by him. _____
2. This book was checked out by my sister, but I read it. _____
3. The landlord repaired the bathroom ceiling after a leak was reported by the tenants. _____
4. The boat lost its rudder, and the Coast Guard had to tow it to shore. _____
5. Smoking was given up by her because her mother was worried about it. _____
6. Julie Andrews had a beautiful voice, but her singing career was stopped by throat surgery. _____
7. My paper was nearly finished until my computer was walked on by my cat. _____
8. The factory workers complained about conditions, but the union was not joined by them. _____
9. Land mines injure hundreds of people every year, so a campaign to stop their use was started by her. _____
10. The contestants jumped in a pool of sewage, and a lot of money was won by one of them. _____

Name ______________________________ Section ____________ Date ____________

## ◆ 18.1 Identifying Dangling Modifiers

For help with this exercise, see sections 18A, 18B, and 18C in *Foundations First*. This exercise is also available online (Exercise Central, Chapter 18, 642).

Decide whether each of the sentences below contains a dangling modifier. If it does, underline the dangling modifier. If the sentence is correct as written, write *C* on the line that follows it.

*Example:* <u>Setting the table</u>, one of the forks was dirty. _____

1. Offered a chance to go to college, the diner seemed like a good way to earn some extra money. _____
2. Working the lunch hour, the staff had to run from place to place. _____
3. Settled in the back booth, the jukebox blared a tune from the 1970s. _____
4. Avoiding the soup of the day, grilled cheese sandwiches were a popular choice. _____
5. Leaving a very small tip, the angry waiter tossed the coins on the floor. _____
6. Slopped all over the floor, the coffee became a slippery hazard. _____
7. Offering refills without being asked, the oldest waiter pleased every customer. _____
8. Smoking in the restroom, the fire alarms went off. _____
9. Emptied without warning, one customer had just gotten his order. _____
10. Finding restaurant work a hard way to make a living, the end of the shift could not come soon enough. _____

Name ____________________ Section __________ Date __________

## ◆ 18.2 Correcting Dangling Modifiers

For help with this exercise, see section 18C in *Foundations First*. This exercise is also available online (Exercise Central, Chapter 18, 643).

Each of the following sentences contains a dangling modifier. Rewrite the sentence so that the modifier refers to the word or word group in parentheses.

*Example:* Watching the game, the popcorn was spilled during an exciting moment. (the fans)

Watching the game, the fans spilled the popcorn during an exciting moment.

1. Buying tickets to the game in advance, plans were made for a night out. (we)

2. Fed and bathed, dinner was eaten early. (the children)

3. Seeing our overheated car on the roadside, a mechanic was telephoned. (a passing motorist)

4. Arriving in a tow truck, the game was being played on the radio. (the mechanic)

5. Watching the game on the garage's small television, our disappointment was shown clearly. (we)

6. Calling a taxi, arrangements were made to get us to the game. (the boss)

7. Driving too fast, the attention of a police officer was attracted. (the taxi)

_______________________________________________

_______________________________________________

8. Pitying our situation, we were sent ahead on foot. (the police officer)

_______________________________________________

_______________________________________________

9. Taking our tickets, it was said that the game was half over. (the gatekeeper)

_______________________________________________

_______________________________________________

10. Forgetting everything that had happened on the way, hot dogs and drinks were purchased. (we)

_______________________________________________

_______________________________________________

Name ______________________ Section __________ Date __________

## ◆ 18.3 Identifying Misplaced Modifiers

For help with this exercise, see sections 18A, 18B, and 18D in *Foundations First*. This exercise is also available online (Exercise Central, Chapter 18, 644).

Decide whether each of the sentences below contains a misplaced modifier. If it does, underline the misplaced modifier, and then circle the word or words it is supposed to modify. If the sentence is correct as written, write *C* on the line that follows it.

*Example:* Warned not to open the door to strangers, the little men went to work while (Snow White) stayed at home alone.

_____

1. Made of bricks, the third little pig felt safe in his house. _____
2. With her big teeth, Red Riding Hood hardly recognized her grandmother. _____
3. The tortoise defeated the hare in the race moving slowly and steadily. _____
4. Finding his bowl empty, the baby bear asked for more porridge. _____
5. Cinderella wept over missing the ball at the palace left behind in a ragged dress. _____
6. Pinocchio's nose proved that he had told a lie growing longer every minute. _____
7. The princess could not sleep at all with a pea under her mattress. _____
8. After rubbing the lamp three times, a genie appeared to Aladdin. _____
9. Having slept for twenty years, Rip van Winkle did not recognize anyone he met. _____
10. Lost and hungry, the gingerbread house looked delicious to Hansel and Gretel. _____

Name ______________________ Section __________ Date __________

## ◆ 18.4 Correcting Misplaced Modifiers

For help with this exercise, see section 18D in *Foundations First*. This exercise is also available online (Exercise Central, Chapter 18, 645).

Rewrite each sentence so that the modifier clearly refers to the word it logically modifies.

*Example:* He opened the door for the plumber wearing a bathrobe covered with happy faces.

Wearing a bathrobe covered with happy faces, he opened the door for the plumber.

1. Clogging the drain, the plumber attempted to remove the debris.

2. The chihuahua darted around the plumber's feet full of energy.

3. Waving a wrench, the dog avoided the annoyed plumber.

4. Covered with shampoo, the hot water in the shower poured onto my head.

5. Cutting off the water main, I yelled for the plumber to stop.

6. Barking furiously, the plumber could not hear me over the chihuahua.

7. I waited for the water to come out of the faucet shivering in the chilly shower stall.

_______________________________________________

_______________________________________________

8. The plumber went to get some lunch with no knowledge of my predicament.

_______________________________________________

_______________________________________________

9. I finally stormed out in search of the plumber pulling on my robe and bunny slippers.

_______________________________________________

_______________________________________________

10. Filling with soap, the chihuahua disappeared in front of my eyes.

_______________________________________________

_______________________________________________

Name ______________________________ Section ____________ Date ____________

## ◆ 19.1 Using Regular Verbs in the Past Tense

For help with this exercise, see section 19A in *Foundations First.* This exercise is also available online (Exercise Central, Chapter 19, 646).

In each of the following sentences, write the past tense form of the verb in parentheses.

*Example:* The original Monopoly game (use) __used__ the names of streets in Atlantic City, New Jersey.

1. Charles Darrow first (approach) _________ Parker Brothers with his board game Monopoly in 1933.
2. With an amazing lack of foresight, the company (reject) _________ the game.
3. The company (complain) _________ that the game was too long and confusing.
4. Darrow was (disappoint) _________ but not defeated.
5. The game inventor (create) _________ five thousand sets on his own and sold them to a Philadelphia department store.
6. After the game was a Christmas sell-out, Parker Brothers (change) _________ its mind and bought Darrow's game.
7. Monopoly (earn) _________ millions of dollars for both Charles Darrow and Parker Brothers.
8. One game of Monopoly (last) _________ for seventy days—the record so far.
9. A Braille version of the famous game (appear) _________ in the 1970s.
10. The game of Monopoly (succeed) _________ because it is both fun and challenging.

Name ______________________ Section __________ Date __________

## ◆ 19.2 Using Irregular Verbs in the Past Tense

For help with this exercise, see section 19B in *Foundations First.* This exercise is also available online (Exercise Central, Chapter 19, 647).

Use the list of irregular verbs on page 000 to find the correct past tense form of the irregular verb in parentheses. In each of the following sentences, write the past tense form of the boldface verb in the space provided.

*Example:* The alarm (ring) ___rang___ but I didn't hear it.

1. That morning I (sleep) _________ blissfully through my first class.
2. When I finally (awake) _________, it was almost 9 o'clock.
3. I (throw) _________ on some clothes and grabbed my book bag.
4. I (drive) _________ to a nearby fast-food restaurant for a take-out breakfast.
5. When I arrived at school, I (find) _________ that the elevator was out of order.
6. With all the energy I could muster, I (spring) _________ up the stairs just in time for Spanish class.
7. Unfortunately, the instructor (choose) _________ me to read a dialogue aloud with another student.
8. I (think) _________ my pronunciation was terrible, but the teacher said I was improving.
9. At the language lab, I (spend) _________ an hour working on the day's assignment.
10. After lunch, I (leave) _________ for my job, where I arrived early to make up for the morning's bad start.

Name ______________________ Section __________ Date __________

## ◆ 19.3 Using the Past Tense of *Be*

For help with this exercise, see section 19C in *Foundations First.* This exercise is also available online (Exercise Central, Chapter 19, 648).

Complete each of the following sentences by choosing the correct past tense form of the verb *be*. Write *was* or *were* in the space provided.

*Example:* Bessie Coleman __was__ the first African-American female pilot.

1. Bessie Coleman ________ born poor, black, and female in a small town in Texas in the early 1900s.
2. Bessie ________ forced to drop out of high school to help support her family.
3. Her dream ________ to go to college and make something of her life.
4. She decided that her problems ________ not going to stop her.
5. Finally, this hard-working young woman ________ able to move to Chicago and get a good job.
6. Becoming a pilot ________ her new ambition.
7. In the 1920s, no African Americans ________ admitted to American flight schools, so Bessie got her pilot's license in France.
8. African-American organizations ________ proud of Bessie's achievements and gave her many honors.
9. Her airplane stunts ________ attended by hundreds of African-American and white fans.
10. Bessie Coleman's example ________ an inspiration to generations of young black pilots, both male and female.

Name ______________________________ Section __________ Date __________

## ◆ 19.4 Using the Past Tense of *Can* and *Will*

For help with this exercise, see section 19D in *Foundations First.* This exercise is also available online (Exercise Central, Chapter 19, 649).

Complete each of the following sentences by choosing the correct form of the verb in parentheses.

*Example:* I thought I (will, would) __would__ like the movie, but I didn't.

1. Madison (can, could) _________ read a few words even though she is only three years old.
2. Roger told his employer that he (can, could) _________ work late that day.
3. The tour guide explained that the trip to the museum (will, would) _________ take about three hours.
4. Anyone who has athletic ability and a good academic record (can, could) _________ apply for this scholarship.
5. Melanie is hoping that Tyler (will, would) _________ bring binoculars to the football game.
6. Jamal (will, would) _________ like to buy a reliable, inexpensive used car.
7. The mechanic assured Aisha that he (can, could) _________ fix her brakes by Tuesday.
8. (Will, Would) you accept a lower salary if the job were especially interesting?
9. I wish I (can, could) _________ figure out what's bothering her.
10. Any animal (will, would) _________ protect its young if they were attacked.

Name ______________________ Section ____________ Date ____________

## ◆ 20.1 Using Regular Past Participles

For help with this exercise, see section 20A in *Foundations First.* This exercise is also available online (Exercise Central, Chapter 20, 650).

Fill in the correct past participle form of each verb in parentheses.

*Example:* My hectic schedule has (tire) ___tired___ me out.

1. I have (attend) _________ classes for fifteen hours each week this semester.
2. Every weekday night, I have (study) _________ for three hours.
3. To keep fit, I have (work) _________ out three times a week at the gym.
4. Since staying healthy is important, I have (prepare) _________ nutritious meals for myself.
5. Well, sometimes I have (cheat) _________ by going to a fast-food restaurant for a tasty burger and fries.
6. I have (swallow) _________ a huge amount of vitamins.
7. My father has (praise) _________ my ability to do well in school while holding down a part-time job.
8. My mother has (contribute) _________ to my well-being by occasionally doing my laundry.
9. However, I have (insist) _________ on cleaning my own room.
10. My room, unfortunately, has (remain) _________ a disaster area.

Name ______________________________ Section ____________ Date ____________

## ◆ 20.2 Using Irregular Past Participles

For help with this exercise, see section 20B in *Foundations First.* This exercise is also available online (Exercise Central, Chapter 20, 651).

Fill in the correct past participle form of each verb in parentheses.

*Example:* Lack of sleep has (become) __become__ a problem for millions of Americans.

1. Insomnia, or sleep problems, have (lead) _________ many to ask their doctors for medication.
2. However, sleeping pills have (hurt) _________ insomniacs by making them dependent on drugs for sleep.
3. Many people with sleep problems have (choose) _________ more natural methods of getting more sleep.
4. Some have (find) _________ that they sleep better if they exercise for thirty minutes several hours before bedtime.
5. Others have (sleep) _________ better after reading or listening to quiet music.
6. Poor sleepers have (go) _________ to bed only when they felt sleepy.
7. When they have (awake) _________ during the night, they have done some light work until they were sleepy again.
8. People with sleep problems have (give) _________ up naps so that they will be sleepy at night.
9. Some insomniacs have (teach) _________ themselves to meditate during the day to relieve stress.
10. If sleep problems have (keep) _________ you from feeling rested, try some of these techniques.

Name ______________________________ Section __________ Date __________

## ◆ 20.3 Using the Past and Present Perfect Tenses

For help with this exercise, see section 20C in *Foundations First.* This exercise is also available online (Exercise Central, Chapter 20, 652).

Fill in the appropriate tense (past or present perfect) of the verb in parentheses.

*Example:* Holly ___was___ (be) a teenager in the 1960s.

1. She remembers that she _________ (wear) bell-bottomed jeans and tie-dyed shirts.
2. She and her friends in high school _________ (listen) to the Beatles, the Who, and The Band.
3. They all _________ (hope) to go to the Woodstock Festival, but none of them actually got there.
4. Later, she _________ (go) to college, became a teacher, married, and had a daughter.
5. Now, Holly _________ (become) the grandmother of two adorable girls.
6. Through the years, she _________ (remain) a lover of rock music.
7. These days, the Dave Mathews Band and U2 _________ (become) two of her favorite bands.
8. Last month, she _________ (attend) concerts by Ani DiFranco and Macy Gray.
9. Holly _________ (collect) the musical recordings of her favorite groups from the 1960s through the present.
10. Her old records are worth money, but she _________ (be) reluctant to sell them.

Name ______________________ Section __________ Date __________

## ◆ 20.4 Using the Present Perfect and Past Perfect Tenses

For help with this exercise, see sections 20C and 20D in *Foundations First.* This exercise is also available online (Exercise Central, Chapter 20, 653).

Complete each of the following sentences by choosing the correct form of the verb in parentheses.

*Example:* The Palmyra Atoll, a group of fifty-two small islands in the Pacific Ocean, (has been, had been) ___has been___ a territory of the United States for many years.

1. Some people claimed that in 1816 pirates (have buried, had buried) __________ treasure on one of the islands.

2. For years, the U.S. Navy (has maintained, had maintained) __________ an airport for its planes there, but that is gone.

3. By the 1970s, the U.S. Energy Department (has proposed, had proposed) __________ that nuclear waste be dumped on these uninhabited islands.

4. Until recently, a private owner (has kept, had kept) __________ control of the islands for many years.

5. Investors (have offered, had offered) __________ to build a hotel and casino, but the owner refused.

6. By 2000, the owner (has sold, had sold) __________ these fifty-two islands to a nature conservation organization.

7. This group bought the islands because it (has feared, had feared) __________ that their natural beauty would be ruined.

8. These nature lovers (have promised, had promised) __________ to protect the plants, animals, and coral reefs on the islands forever.

9. Since the islands were sold, scientists (have studied, had studied) _____________ the plants and seabirds that thrive there.

10. Tourists (have awaited, had awaited) _____________ permission to visit these islands, but the nature group is not eager to have them.

Name ______________________ Section __________ Date __________

## ◆ 20.5 Using the Past and Past Perfect Tenses

For help with this exercise, see section 20D in *Foundations First*. This exercise is also available online (Exercise Central, Chapter 20, 654).

Complete each of the following sentences by choosing the correct form of the verb in parentheses.

*Example:* By the time the party was over, they (ate, had eaten) ___had eaten___ all the doughnuts and chocolate chip cookies.

1. Doughnuts (were, had been) ______________ invented by bakers in Holland in the sixteenth century.
2. Before they were called doughnuts, they (were, had been) ______________ named "oil cakes."
3. The Pilgrims came to America after they (spent, had spent) ______________ years in Holland.
4. They (brought, had brought) ______________ these oil cakes, which had no holes.
5. After a while, Americans (gave, had given) ______________ the name "dough nut" to these cakes because they were the size of a walnut.
6. The hole in the doughnut's center was the result of an incident that (occurred, had occurred) ______________ in the mid-1900s.
7. After a sea captain from Maine (poked, had poked) ______________ a hole in his mother's doughnuts, the idea caught on.
8. Chocolate chip cookies (were, had been) ______________ invented by an American woman, Ruth Wakefield.

9. She (was, had been) _____________ the cook and baker at the Toll House Inn in New England.

10. Mrs. Wakefield (added, had added) _____________ chocolate chunks to her cookie recipe before anyone else ever thought of the idea.

Name ______________________________ Section __________ Date __________

## ◆ 20.6 Using Past Participles as Adjectives

For help with this exercise, see section 20E in *Foundations First.* This exercise is also available online (Exercise Central, Chapter 20, 655).

The following sentences contain errors in past participle forms used as adjectives. Cross out any underlined participle that is incorrect, and write the correct form in the blank. If the participle form is correct, write *C* in the blank.

*Example:* The children were frighten __frightened__ by the scary movie.

1. Bake ____________ chips are less fattening than chips fried in oil.
2. The expensive vase is broke ____________ and cannot be repaired.
3. Some grown ____________ people enjoy playing marbles as much as kids do.
4. The football player seemed unconcern ____________ about his injury.
5. Whenever my sister feels hurt ____________ , she goes to her room and sulks.
6. The fallen ____________ tree blocked the driveway of their house.
7. The hole in the wore ____________ carpet was covered by a throw rug.
8. The driver became alarm ____________ when she saw a deer in the road ahead.
9. As the air leaked out of the balloon, the toddler looked surprised ____________.
10. Add a beat ____________ egg to the cake mix.

Name ______________________________ Section ____________ Date ____________

## ◆ 20.7 Using Past Participles as Adjectives

For help with this exercise, see section 20E in *Foundations First.* This exercise is also available online (Exercise Central, Chapter 20, 656).

In the following pairs of sentences, the underlined past participle is used as an adjective after a linking verb. Combine the two sentences into one longer sentence, with the past participle modifying the noun that follows it.

*Example:* The toast was burned. We had to throw it out.

We had to throw out the burned toast.

1. The vegetables were roasted. Bert served them with rice.

2. In this office, we keep confidential papers in a file cabinet. The cabinet is locked.

3. The child's dress was torn. Her mother repaired it.

4. The plumber was licensed. He knew how to fix the leaky pipe.

5. White wine is chilled. It is often served with dessert.

6. The protesters were determined. They marched to the state capitol.

7. Mr. Lopez is certified. He is a teacher of mathematics.

8. The mistake was in the last paragraph. It was <u>unnoticed</u>.

______________________________________________

______________________________________________

9. The candle was <u>lit</u>. It quickly sputtered out.

______________________________________________

______________________________________________

10. Our door was <u>stuck</u>. We opened it with a kick.

______________________________________________

______________________________________________

Name ______________________ Section __________ Date __________

## ◆ 21.1 Forming Noun Plurals

For help with this exercise, see section 21C in *Foundations First.* This exercise is also available online (Exercise Central, Chapter 21, 657).

Proofread the underlined nouns in the following sentences. Check the nouns for correct plural form. If a correction needs to be made, cross out the noun and write the correct form above it. If the noun is correct, write *C* above it.

*Example:* Cars, trains, planes, and ~~busses~~ (buses) transport our family members (C) to the annual Thanksgiving gathering.

1. Our Thanksgiving dinners involve several families contributing to one huge meal.
2. My brother Bernie and sister-in-law Alice and their children, Sabrina, Adam, and Michael, all create special dishs.
3. The daughter-in-laws, Debra and Jennifer, wifes of Adam and Michael, specialize in pies and other desserts.
4. Sabrina bakes loafs of fresh bread.
5. Guests arrive with many varieties of cranberry sauce, vegetable mixs, and sweet potatos.
6. Several cousines and their brothers-in-law and sisters-in-law are among the guests.
7. As turkeys go, our turkey is big because it must feed thirty persons.
8. Dinner is a long and noisy affair, complete with the crys of babys.
9. Before dinner, the host and hostess give speechs of welcome and thanksgiving.
10. After dinner, storys and jokes are told and the latest family photos are passed around.

Name ______________________________ Section __________ Date __________

## ◆ 22.1 Identifying Pronoun Antecedents

For help with this exercise, see section 22B in *Foundations First.* This exercise is also available online (Exercise Central, Chapter 22, 658).

In each of the following sentences, a pronoun is underlined. In the blank after each sentence, write the noun that is the antecedent of the underlined pronoun.

*Example:* Women fought for years so that <u>they</u> could vote and hold public office. ___Women___

1. When Elizabeth Cady Stanton was young, <u>she</u> realized that girls were considered less important than boys. ______________
2. In the mid-1800s women had few legal rights, and <u>they</u> were under the control of their fathers or husbands. ______________
3. Elizabeth's father, a respected judge, wished that <u>she</u> had been a boy. ______________
4. After attending a women's college, Elizabeth married Henry Stanton and <u>they</u> had children. ______________
5. Elizabeth and her husband were abolitionists who hated slavery and fought against <u>it</u>. ______________
6. While women were protesting slavery, <u>they</u> began to fight for women's rights. ______________
7. After the Civil War, black men had the vote, but women of all races did not have <u>it</u>. ______________
8. The struggle to give women the vote took many years, and <u>it</u> faced much opposition. ______________
9. A person opposed to votes for women would say that <u>he or she</u> believed that women did not belong in the rough world of politics. ______________
10. People who supported votes for women argued that <u>they</u> had the same right to vote as men did. ______________

Name ______________________ Section __________ Date __________

## ◆ 22.2 Understanding Pronoun-Antecedent Agreement

For help with this exercise, see section 22B in *Foundations First.* This exercise is also available online (Exercise Central, Chapter 22, 659).

Complete each of the following sentences by writing the correct pronoun in the blank.

*Example:* Our school sent ___its___ baseball team to visit the Baseball Hall of Fame in Cooperstown, New York.

1. When the players arrived at the Baseball Hall of Fame, _________ couldn't wait to get in.
2. Cooperstown is in northwestern New York, and _________ had been the home of Abner Doubleday.
3. Abner Doubleday claimed that _________ had invented baseball in 1839 in Cooperstown.
4. However, a similar game had been played in America since colonial times, and _________ was probably the game Doubleday and his friends played.
5. In this game, called "rounders," a player hit a ball with a bat and then ran around bases while fielders tried to hit _________ with the ball.
6. Alexander Cartwright set down the rules of baseball in 1845, and all teams now follow _________.
7. Visitors to the Baseball Hall of Fame can view exhibits that explain the history of baseball to _________.
8. When I saw the first catcher's mask, used in 1876, it looked like a bird cage to _________.
9. Interactive videos at the museum introduce each Hall of Famer and tell about _________ life.
10. The World Series room was my favorite, and _________ was full of interesting information.

Name ______________________ Section __________ Date __________

## ◆ 22.3 Understanding Pronoun-Antecedent Agreement with Compound Antecedents

For help with this exercise, see section 22C in *Foundations First.* This exercise is also available online (Exercise Central, Chapter 22, 660).

The following sentences contain errors in pronoun reference with compound antecedents. Decide whether each underlined pronoun is correct. If it is not, cross out the pronoun and write the correct pronoun above it. If it is correct, label it *C.*

*Example:* I liked the book *Harry Potter* better than the movie because ~~they~~ it had more details.

1. The film and the book may be similar, or it may be very different.
2. The filmmakers who produced *Harry Potter* and *Lord of the Rings* both followed their sources as closely as possible.
3. The author or screenwriter had to cut some of the episodes even if they didn't want to.
4. My brother and I enjoyed the books and the films, but we thought that they were different.
5. When I read *Lord of the Rings,* I imagined what the characters looked like, and it became real to me.
6. But when I saw a live actor or actress in the film, they changed my image of the character.
7. When my brother saw places and events from *Harry Potter,* he was more fascinated with it than I was.
8. I thought that the filmed scenery and action were interesting, but it took away the fun of imagining.
9. A book may contain beautiful descriptions and witty observations, but they are often lost in the film version.
10. Many people who have read the books will see *Harry Potter* or *Lord of the Rings* during their run in movie theaters or on video.

Name ________________________________ Section ___________ Date ___________

## ◆ 22.4 Understanding Pronoun-Antecedent Agreement with Indefinite Pronouns

For help with this exercise, see section 22C in *Foundations First.* This exercise is also available online (Exercise Central, Chapter 22, 661).

In the following passage, fill in each blank with the correct pronoun. Then draw an arrow from the pronoun in the blank to its indefinite pronoun antecedent.

*Example:* Everyone has a special talent or ability that he or she should cultivate.

1. Each of us has _________ talent or ability, whether it is in sports, music, the arts, or in dealing with other people.
2. Nobody should ignore _________ special gift or think it is not as valuable as someone else's.
3. For example, few become famous for _________ athletic, musical, or acting ability, but the rest of us can still get pleasure from these activities.
4. No one should give up an enjoyable activity because _________ thinks that other people are more talented at it.
5. Everything we do to the best of our ability has _________ purpose.
6. Someone who is a creative cook gives _________ family and friends a much-appreciated gift.
7. Neither Darlene, who writes poetry, or Stan, who writes science fiction stories, has ever had _________ writing published.
8. Still, both of them enjoy writing and sharing _________ creations with friends.
9. Others find that _________ talent is for leadership and become coaches, scout leaders, teachers, or community leaders.
10. Another might contribute _________ talent to the community by doing volunteer home repairs or gardening.

Name ______________________ Section __________ Date __________

## ◆ 22.5 Avoiding Vague Pronouns

For help with this exercise, see section 22D in *Foundations First.* This exercise is also available online (Exercise Central, Chapter 22, 662).

The following sentences contain vague and unnecessary pronouns. Rewrite each sentence correctly on the lines below it.

*Example:* On TV, it said that we will be getting six to eight inches of snow tonight.

The TV weather reporter said that we will be getting six to eight inches of snow tonight.

1. My brother, he just got a job as a computer programmer at an insurance company.

2. In the instructions, it explained how to connect the television set and the VCR.

3. In the school library, they provide lots of help with research.

4. My aerobics instructor, she gives us a good workout.

5. At the Hershey, Pennsylvania, museum, they have an interesting exhibit about how chocolate is made.

6. At the mall, they are having some terrific sales this weekend.

7. The party that I was looking forward to, it turned out to be pretty boring.

8. This sweater, it had a rip in it that I didn't notice when I bought it.

9. The dog, he looks forward to his walk every day.

10. On the radio, it said that gasoline prices are going up.

Name ________________ Section ________ Date ________

## ◆ 22.6 Understanding Pronoun Case

For help with this exercise, see section 22E in *Foundations First.* This exercise is also available online (Exercise Central, Chapter 22, 663).

Fill in the blank with the correct form of the personal pronoun in each sentence.

*Example:* Sarah loves to sing and so do I. ___She___ and I sing together often.

1. My brother Adam plays the clarinet, and I play piano. ________ and I often play duets.
2. He likes classical music more than ________.
3. When we go to a concert, he explains a lot of things about the music to ________.
4. On the other hand, I know more about jazz than ________.
5. Music is a passion with ________ musicians.
6. Our father plays the violin, and he is a more experienced musician than ________, his children, are.
7. Dad took Adam and ________ to concerts when we were very young.
8. Dad was also part of a string quartet of four musicians. ________ often practiced at our house.
9. As kids, we loved listening to ________ play and often fell asleep to the beautiful music.
10. Adam and ________ plan to bring up our own children to enjoy all kinds of music.

Name ______________________________ Section __________ Date __________

## ◆ 22.7 Understanding Pronoun Case: Compounds

For help with this exercise, see section 22F in *Foundations First.* This exercise is also available online (Exercise Central, Chapter 22, 664).

In each blank, write the correct form (subjective or objective) of the pronouns in parentheses.

*Example:* ___I___ Derek and (I, me) are the stars of the basketball team.

1. The award for outstanding community service was given to Felice Chang and _________ (I, me).
2. We invited Serena and _________ (he, him) to the graduation party, but only Serena showed up.
3. _________ (He, Him) and his girlfriend had a big fight last Friday.
4. The police officer charged that _________ (they, them) and their barking dogs were disturbing the peace.
5. Many people think that _________ (she, her) and _________ (I, me) look very much alike.
6. No one in the neighborhood likes _________ (he, him) or his brother.
7. _________ (They, Them) and _________ (I, me) went to every football game this season.
8. This argument is between _________ (he, him) and _________ (I, me), so don't interfere.
9. Going out to dinner and a movie has always been a favorite date for _________ (he, him) and _________ (she, her).
10. My best friend and _________ (I, me) have known each other since third grade.

Name ______________________________ Section ____________ Date ____________

## ◆ 22.8 Understanding Pronoun Case: Comparisons

For help with this exercise, see section 22F in *Foundations First.* This exercise is also available online (Exercise Central, Chapter 22, 665).

In each blank, write the correct form (subjective or objective) of the pronouns in parentheses. In brackets, add the word or words needed to complete the comparison.

*Example:* Ben is much more sentimental than __I [am]__ (I, me).

1. No one is more driven to succeed than _________ (she, her).
2. Anthony was as good a runner as Kareem, but Kareem was a better batter than _________ (he, him).
3. Doing poorly on the midterm bothered Seema as much as _________ (I, me).
4. Jackie believes the stories people tell her more easily than _________ (I, me).
5. Horror movies frighten you more than _________ (we, us).
6. The trip to the theme park was more fun for you than _________ (they, them).
7. Tyler plays the saxophone better than _________ (I, me).
8. Living in a foreign country affected Victor as much as _________ (she, her).
9. Leasing a new minivan is costing you more than _________ (we, us).
10. He likes pizza more than _________ (I, me) and always eats more slices.

Name ______________________ Section __________ Date __________

## ◆ 22.9 Understanding Pronoun Case: *Who, Whom*

For help with this exercise, see section 22F in *Foundations First.* This exercise is also available online (Exercise Central, Chapter 22, 666).

Complete each of the following sentences by circling either *who* or *whom* in parentheses.

*Example:* Renee, for (who, whom) the day is not long enough, often goes to bed exhausted.

1. Are you one of those people (who, whom) are exhausted at the end of the day?
2. If you are someone to (who, whom) tiredness is a problem, you are not alone.
3. There are many adults (who, whom) suffer from fatigue, even though they are otherwise healthy.
4. A person for (who, whom) getting enough sleep is a struggle is likely to get tired easily.
5. Anyone (who, whom) has interrupted sleep won't have enough energy to get through the day.
6. People (who, whom) drink too much water in the evening will probably get up several times during the night.
7. Those (who, whom) drink alcohol before bedtime will not get a good night's sleep.
8. Many for (who, whom) low blood pressure is a problem feel tired all day.
9. Almost everyone (who, whom) has either thyroid problems or anemia may suffer from fatigue also.
10. Students (who, whom) strain their eyes reading or using the computer are often tired during exam periods.

Name ______________________________ Section ____________ Date ____________

## ◆ 22.10 Understanding Intensive and Reflexive Pronouns

For help with this exercise, see section 22G in *Foundations First.* This exercise is also available online (Exercise Central, Chapter 22, 667).

Complete each of the following sentences by filling in the correct reflexive or intensive pronoun.

*Example:* The coach told the players, "Get ___yourselves___ ready for a tough game."

1. Claudia treated ______________ to a new sweater on payday.
2. An engaged couple should give ______________ time to get to know each other before marriage.
3. Doug ______________ had no idea who had sent him the e-mail.
4. We found ______________ on a scenic road that we had never traveled before.
5. You ______________ told me that this plan would work.
6. I try to pace ______________ when I exercise so that I don't get tired too quickly.
7. Pierre convinced ______________ that the car accident could not have been avoided.
8. The snake coiled ______________ up and prepared to strike.
9. The president of the college, Dr. Juanita Martin, ______________ handed out the diplomas to the graduates.
10. You all should remind ______________ how lucky you are to be so healthy.

Name ______________________ Section __________ Date __________

## ◆ 23.1 Using Adjectives and Adverbs

For help with this exercise, see section 23A in *Foundations First.* This exercise is also available online (Exercise Central, Chapter 23, 668).

In the following passage, circle the correct form (adjective or adverb) from the choices in parentheses.

*Example:* Nature sometimes treats human beings (violent, violently).

1. Earthquakes, hurricanes, tornadoes, and volcanoes are all (serious, seriously) threats to human life and property.
2. Fortunately, most earthquakes are (real, really) mild and cause little damage.
3. However, earthquakes not only topple buildings and break pipelines, but also cause (destructive, destructively) fires.
4. California has had serious earthquakes, but (practical, practically) every part of the country has had mild ones.
5. Hurricanes are storms hundreds of miles wide that (frequent, frequently) threaten tropical regions.
6. The natives of the West Indies called these storms "evil winds," and hurricanes often behave (evil, evilly).
7. Tornadoes are smaller storms that do their damage (local, locally).
8. (Near, Nearly) all residents of the midwestern part of the United States know about the power of tornadoes.
9. Mount St. Helens in Washington State was a volcano that was not (active, actively) for many years.
10. But in 1980, the volcano (unexpected, unexpectedly) erupted and caused widespread damage.

Name ________________________ Section ____________ Date ____________

## ◆ 23.2 Using *Good* and *Well*

For help with this exercise, see section 23A in *Foundations First.* This exercise is also available online (Exercise Central, Chapter 23, 669).

In the following passage, circle the correct form (*good* or *well*) from the choices in parentheses.

*Example:* A natural disaster is never a (good, well) experience, but you can survive (good, well) if you are prepared.

1. You can survive a disaster such as an earthquake or flood if you have prepared (good, well) in advance.
2. First of all, keep a (good, well) stock of canned and dried food and bottled water in your house.
3. Buy flashlights and batteries, matches, and candles that will give you a (good, well) light by which to do everyday tasks.
4. A portable outdoor grill for cooking will ensure that you eat (good, well).
5. For the cold weather, have a source of heat, such as a kerosene heater, that works (good, well) and does not require electricity.
6. It would be a (good, well) idea to have a transistor radio with batteries so that you can hear instructions from public officials.
7. Finally, a supply of medicines and a first-aid kit will help you and your family feel (good, well).
8. You would do (good, well) to have a survival kit in your car, too.
9. In order to be prepared for an escape by car from a disaster area, have a (good, well) supply of food, bottled water, warm clothing, and blankets in the car.
10. A fire extinguisher, flares, a flashlight, and a first-aid kit will keep you (good-, well-) protected in emergencies.

Name ______________________ Section __________ Date __________

## ◆ 23.3 Using Comparatives and Superlatives

For help with this exercise, see section 23B in *Foundations First.* This exercise is also available online (Exercise Central, Chapter 23, 670).

Fill in the correct comparative or superlative form of the word or words in parentheses.

*Example:* What do you think is the <u>most important</u> (more important, most important) thing in life?

1. Julia Butterfly Hill is __________ (more idealistic, idealisticer) than most people.
2. She is also __________ (stronger, more stronger) than she ever thought she was.
3. She has been willing to endure some of the __________ (worse, worst) experiences a person can in order to fight for her beliefs.
4. Julia is an environmental activist who volunteered to live in one of the __________ (biggest, most biggest) trees in the California redwood forest.
5. Although she was __________ (most frightened, more frightened) of heights than she thought, Julia lived on a six-by-six-foot platform in the tree.
6. During the first three months, her __________ (greatest, most greatest) fear was that loggers might cut down the tree with her in it.
7. This did not happen, but __________ (upsettinger, more upsetting) things did in the 738 days she spent in the tree.
8. Among the __________ (scariest, most scariest) tactics used by her opponents was buzzing her tree with a helicopter and blowing an airhorn for eight days and eight nights.

9. Ms. Hill was able to survive rainstorms with 90-mile-an-hour winds and only became ___________________ (determineder, more determined) to save the redwoods from loggers.

10. Her ___________________ (most happy, happiest) moment was when the logging company promised to spare redwoods within a 200-foot-wide zone.

Name ______________________________ Section __________ Date __________

## ◆ 23.4 Using the Comparative and Superlative of *Good/Well* and *Bad/Badly*

For help with this exercise, see section 23B in *Foundations First.* This exercise is also available online (Exercise Central, Chapter 23, 671).

Fill in the correct comparative or superlative form of the word or words in parentheses.

*Example:* Some days are much __worse__ (bad) than others.

1. The _________ (bad) day I've had in a long time was last Friday.
2. Usually, I look forward to Friday as the _________ (good) day of my week.
3. The weekend is the time when I can relax, have fun, and feel _________ (well) than I do most weekdays.
4. That Friday morning, I was running late and then tried my _________ (good) to get to work on time.
5. I thought I wasn't speeding, but the police officer knew _________ (good) and gave me a ticket.
6. I arrived very late at my office and felt even _________ (badly) when I discovered that my computer was down.
7. Next I looked at my sales record, which was the _________ (bad) it had ever been.
8. After that, I spilled a cup of coffee on my new suit, which only made things _________ (bad).
9. I had never had a _________ (bad) day, so I closed my office door and tried to relax.
10. Twenty minutes later, I felt _________ (well), and I treated myself to lunch out with a friend.

Name ______________________ Section __________ Date __________

## ◆ 23.5 Using Demonstrative Adjectives

For help with this exercise, see section 23C in *Foundations First*. This exercise is also available online (Exercise Central, Chapter 23, 672).

In the following passage, circle the correct form of the demonstrative adjective in parentheses.

*Example:* (That, (Those)) schools in the Old West were very rough and challenging.

1. Frontier schools were crowded, noisy, and poorly equipped, and (that, those) problems could be overwhelming for teachers.
2. A typical frontier schoolhouse was a log cabin built by (that, those) parents in the community who wanted a school.
3. The school was often used as a church on Sundays, and (this, these) two uses made the building doubly valuable.
4. There was usually only one teacher for all the children, and (this, these) might range from seven to sixteen years old.
5. The teacher went from (this, these) small group to (that, those) one, helping children learn reading, writing, and arithmetic.
6. Since there were few textbooks, students brought (that, those) books they had at home.
7. (That, Those) boy might be reading an almanac while (this, these) girl learns to read from the family Bible.
8. Other subjects taught at (this, these) schools included American history and geography, penmanship, and spelling.
9. Most youngsters had many farm chores to do and attended school only when (that, those) chores were done.
10. School might be held only during the three or four months of winter, and (this, these) schooling was often the only education a child received.

Name ______________________ Section ____________ Date ____________

## ◆ 24.1 Avoiding Special Problems with Subjects

For help with this exercise, see sections 24A, B, and C in *Foundations First*. This exercise is also available online (Exercise Central, Chapter 24, 673).

Read the following passage, which contains errors in the use of subjects. Check each underlined word or phrase. If it is not used correctly, cross it out and write the correct word or phrase above the line. If the underlined word or phrase is correct, write *C* above it. The first error has been corrected for you.

a goat farm

~~A goat farm~~ I thought ~~it~~ would be a smelly place. (1) Was surprised when I visited a local goat farm where goat cheese is produced. (2) Because there is straw in the goat pens, don't have a bad odor. In addition, the pens are kept very clean, as is the place where the goats get milked. (3) Get milked twice a day and give an average of seven pounds of milk. (4) Is an art to make goat cheese. The milk is pasteurized to kill germs, and special bacteria are added to change the milk to cheese. (5) Rennet is another ingredient and is added to the milk to congeal it or form curds. (6) Whey, a watery by-product, is left when the solid cheese is removed. (7) Is fed to cows on another farm. (8) Goats, they must be kept healthy. (9) The owner of the farm doesn't like visitors because might be carrying disease. (10) The goats are well-treated and even have individual name. No wonder the cheese made from their milk is so delicious.

Name ____________________ Section __________ Date __________

## ◆ 24.2 Understanding Count and Noncount Nouns

For help with this exercise, see section 24D in *Foundations First.* This exercise is also available online (Exercise Central, Chapter 24, 674).

In each of the following sentences, identify the underlined word as a count or noncount noun. If it is a noncount noun, circle the *N* following the sentence, but do not write in the blank. If it is a count noun, circle the *C*, and then write the plural form of the noun in the blank.

*Example:* Mental and physical <u>exercise</u> will help your brain develop.

(N) C ____________

1. You can maximize your <u>intelligence</u> by enhancing the power of your brain.

   N C ____________

2. Playing a mind <u>game</u> such as chess, bridge, or Scrabble and doing crossword puzzles are all good exercises for the brain. N C ____________

3. <u>Memorization</u> keeps the brain sharp, so learn some poems, songs, or quotations by heart. N C ____________

4. Watching television or movies does not help your <u>brain</u> develop because it is not working hard enough. N C ____________

5. Being a <u>student</u> definitely increases your brain power. N C ____________

6. Any kind of mental exercise results in <u>growth</u> of nerve cells and strengthening of the connections between them. N C ____________

7. Physical exercise is a good way to get more blood and <u>oxygen</u> to your brain.

   N C ____________

8. Another way is to eat a low-fat <u>diet</u> so that your arteries stay unclogged.

   N C ____________

9. Keeping physically and mentally healthy is an important <u>tool</u> in brain development. N C ____________

10. On the other hand, <u>stress</u> can create hormones that may actually shrink one's brain. N C ____________

Name ________________________ Section __________ Date __________

## ◆ 24.3 Using Determiners with Count and Noncount Nouns

For help with this exercise, see section 24E in *Foundations First.* This exercise is also available online (Exercise Central, Chapter 24, 675).

In each of the following sentences, circle the appropriate choice from each pair of words or phrases in parentheses.

*Example:* (Many, Much) people get happiness and satisfaction from living with a pet.

1. Cats, dogs, and other pets are part of (many, much) American households.
2. But (a few, a little) people are not able to have pets because they have a physical disability and can't take care of an animal.
3. For (disabled these, these disabled) pet lovers, there is a new solution: robot pets.
4. Although they are made of plastic and computer chips, robot dogs and cats provide (many, much) comfort to their owners.
5. A mechanical pet has a computer brain that allows it to make (a few, a little) decisions on its own.
6. The robots decide where to go and what to do, and this creates (every, enough) "personality" to make them interesting.
7. The robots also develop (a few, a little) habits and even seem to have "feelings."
8. If a robot pet is given (much, many) love and attention, it will treat the owner in the same way.
9. The owner programs the computer inside (each small, small each) robot to make it unique.
10. Owners of robot pets report (few, little) trouble with their pets and say they love them in a special way.

Name ______________________________ Section __________ Date __________

## ◆ 24.4 Understanding Articles

For help with this exercise, see section 24F in *Foundations First.* This exercise is also available online (Exercise Central, Chapter 24, 676).

In the following passage, decide whether each blank space needs a definite article *(the)*, an indefinite article *(a* or *an)*, or no article. If a definite or indefinite article is needed, write it in the space provided. If no article is needed, leave the space blank.

*Example:* When children fall, they can get _a_ scrape.

(1) If your child falls, wash ____ wound as soon as possible with ____ soap and lukewarm water. (2) Look carefully at the cut to see if ____ dirt has gotten in. (3) Children can get ____ abrasion or ____ scraping away of skin and tissue when they fall while ____ skateboarding or ____scootering. (4) Scrub ____ wound with ____ clean towel or washcloth to get all the dirt out. (5) Doctors do not recommend using hydrogen peroxide as ____ antiseptic to clean a wound. (6) Hydrogen peroxide destroys ____ white blood cells that help repair ____ wounds. (7) A better choice is ____ antibiotic ointment that you can buy at any drugstore. (8) The ointment seals ____ wound, and it starts to heal within eight hours, with or without ____ bandage. (9) Put on ____ bandage if the wound is big, bleeds easily, or is rubbing against ____ clothing. (10) Use ____ adhesive bandage or ____ gauze pad, and change ____ covering of the wound every day.

**Name** ______________________ **Section** __________ **Date** __________

## ◆ 24.5 Forming Negative Statements and Questions

For help with this exercise, see section 24G in *Foundations First.* This exercise is also available online (Exercise Central, Chapter 24, 677).

Rewrite each of the following sentences in two ways. First, turn the sentence into a question. Then, rewrite the original sentence as a negative statement.

*Example:* Sydney thought that the movie was outstanding.

Did Sydney think that the movie was outstanding?

Sydney did not think that the movie was outstanding.

1. Erin has finished her term paper.

 ______________________

 ______________________

2. The musicians are playing love songs.

 ______________________

 ______________________

3. The buses leave the terminal every hour.

 ______________________

 ______________________

4. She looked under the bed for her missing shoe.

 ______________________

 ______________________

5. They worried about missing the train.

 ______________________

 ______________________

6. Jed found the stock certificates in the desk.

 ______________________

 ______________________

7. Dinner will be served in the main dining hall.

 ______________________

 ______________________

8. Hashim has been absent for a week.

______________________________________________

______________________________________________

9. Lahela felt proud of winning the swimming event.

______________________________________________

______________________________________________

10. Iliana will meet us at the movie theater.

______________________________________________

______________________________________________

Name ______________________ Section __________ Date __________

## ◆ 24.6 Recognizing Stative Verbs

For help with this exercise, see section 24I in *Foundations First.* This exercise is also available online (Exercise Central, Chapter 24, 678).

In each of the following sentences, first circle the verb. Then correct any problems with stative verbs by crossing out the incorrect verb tense and writing the correct verb tense above the line. If a sentence is correct, write *C* in the blank after the sentence.

*Example:* Leila ~~is desiring~~ desires a job as a newspaper columnist. ____

1. Leila has been writing an opinion column for the college newspaper since September. ____
2. She is loving the experience. ____
3. She has been expressing her ideas about events on campus for months. ____
4. Readers are liking her columns. ____
5. They are wanting to read them every week. ____
6. A few are being critical of her opinions or observations. ____
7. Generally, they are arguing their points politely and rationally. ____
8. Little by little, Leila is becoming a celebrity at school. ____
9. Leila is believing in the free exchange of ideas. ____
10. She now is understanding the power of the press. ____

Name ______________________ Section __________ Date __________

## ◆ 24.7 Placing Adjectives in Order

For help with this exercise, see section 24J in *Foundations First*. This exercise is also available online (Exercise Central, Chapter 24, 679).

Arrange each group of adjectives in the correct order. Then rewrite the complete phrase in the blank.

*Example:* (dark, long, her, beautiful) fingers

her beautiful long dark fingers

1. (annoying, impatient, some) customers

   ______________________________

2. (sentimental, love, this, silly) song

   ______________________________

3. (green, ugly, wool, an) coat

   ______________________________

4. (charming, little, a, country) cottage

   ______________________________

5. (talented, these, rock, young) musicians

   ______________________________

6. (Juanita's, colorful, flower, lovely) paintings

   ______________________________

7. (fluffy, sweet, my, white) cat

   ______________________________

8. (best, the, all, possible) excuses

   ______________________________

9. (blue, sister's, expensive, cashmere, her) sweater

   ______________________________

10. (mischievous, both, twin, dirt-covered) boys

   ______________________________

Name ______________________________ Section __________ Date __________

## ◆ 24.8 Using Prepositions Correctly

For help with this exercise, see sections 24K and 24L in *Foundations First.* This exercise is also available online (Exercise Central, Chapter 24, 680).

In the following passage, fill in each blank with the correct preposition.

*Example:* The following story provides an interesting insight ___into___ how Africans in America held ___onto___ their beliefs and customs.

(1) For three hundred years, Africans were taken _______ their homes _______ the west coast of Africa and brought as slaves _______ America. (2) Over two hundred years ago, an African-American slave buried some objects _______ the basement of a home where she or he lived. (3) The home belonged _______ Charles Carroll and was _______ Annapolis, Maryland. (4) The objects buried included quartz crystals, bone disks, polished stones, and pierced coins. (5) The collection of objects was discovered _______ archaeologists _______ 1991. (6) This group _______ scientists had been digging _______ different places around Annapolis to find out _______ the lives of enslaved and free African Americans. (7) The objects came _______ a region called Kongo that is now part _______ southwest Congo and northern Angola. (8) Kongo parents still put necklaces _______ pierced coins _______ their small children to protect them. (9) In the past, adults wore pierced bone disks _______ their bodies to keep themselves safe. (10) The crystals and polished stones are important _______ the ancient religion _______ the Kongo. (11) The archaeologists who found these objects were amazed _______ how enslaved African Americans managed to keep practicing their ancient religions right _______ the noses of the slaveholders.

Name ______________________ Section __________ Date __________

## ◆ 25.1 Using Commas in a Series

For help with this exercise, see section 25A in *Foundations First.* This exercise is also available online (Exercise Central, Chapter 25, 681).

Edit the following sentences for the correct use of commas in a series. Add commas where needed. If the sentence is correct, write *C* in the blank.

*Example:* Dad bathed the baby, put his pajamas on, and placed him in the crib. ____

1. We ordered a pizza with pepperoni mushrooms anchovies and extra cheese. ____
2. You can wear a dress or a pants suit or a skirt and jacket to the job interview. ____
3. Ginny is cooking the main dish Bruce is making the salad and the twins are setting the table. ____
4. Three movies set in New York City are *Taxi Driver, Wall Street* and *The Godfather.* ____
5. This house has four bedrooms, is equipped with central air-conditioning, and includes a finished basement. ____
6. They brought food, water, mosquito repellent sunscreen, a compass and a map along on the hike. ____
7. Bob collected the money at the door, Tara showed the audience members to their seats and Vinnie acted as master of ceremonies. ____
8. Marissa pinned on the pattern, and cut the cloth, and sewed the skirt in under an hour. ____
9. We can take a bus a train or a cab to the airport. ____
10. Ricky played the saxophone, Antoine was on bass, and Shana sang the vocals. ____

Name ______________________ Section __________ Date __________

## ◆ 25.2 Using Commas to Set off Introductory Phrases

For help with this exercise, see section 25B in *Foundations First.* This exercise is also available online (Exercise Central, Chapter 25, 682).

Edit the following sentences for the correct use of commas with introductory phrases. Add commas where needed. If the sentence is correct, write *C* in the blank.

*Example:* Made into a play and a movie, the story of the Russian princess, Anastasia, still fascinates people. ____

1. During the Bolshevik (Communist) Revolution the Russian czar (ruler) and his family were murdered. ____
2. On the night of July 17, 1918 the royal family was awakened by soldiers of the revolutionary army. ____
3. Along with their private doctor and some servants the family was taken to the basement of a house in which they were staying. ____
4. Once in the basement, they were shot and stabbed with bayonets. ____
5. According to historians two of the bodies were burned, and the other nine were buried. ____
6. Many years later a woman claimed to be Princess Anastasia, who was seventeen at the time of the murders. ____
7. Telling a complicated story the woman insisted that she had been shot but survived. ____
8. For sixty years, the woman tried to convince authorities that she was Anastasia. ____
9. In spite of her efforts they didn't believe her story because she could not speak Russian. ____
10. At the present time Anastasia's body still has not been found. ____

Name ______________________ Section ____________ Date ____________

## ◆ 25.3 Using Commas to Set off Parenthetical Words and Phrases

For help with this exercise, see section 25C in *Foundations First*. This exercise is also available online (Exercise Central, Chapter 22, 683).

Edit the following sentences for the correct use of commas with parenthetical words and phrases. Add commas where needed. If the sentence is correct, write *C* in the blank.

*Example:* The party, of course, was a complete success. ____

1. Lance where did you leave the car keys? ____
2. We can however just stay home and have a quiet evening. ____
3. Instead I'd rather use the money for a vacation. ____
4. That trip to the dentist wasn't so bad, in fact. ____
5. However I hope I don't have to go there again for a long time. ____
6. Celine Dion for example achieved success as a singer at an early age. ____
7. How did you catch the criminal Sherlock Holmes? ____
8. I hope you realize moreover that this is your last chance. ____
9. Mr. Van Allen, unfortunately, is no longer with our organization. ____
10. Consequently his grades began to slide. ____

Name ______________________ Section __________ Date __________

## ◆ 25.4 Using Commas with Appositives

For help with this exercise, see section 25D in *Foundations First.* This exercise is also available online (Exercise Central, Chapter 25, 684).

Edit the following sentences for the correct use of commas to set off appositives. Add commas where needed. If the sentence is correct, write *C* in the blank.

*Example:* Forensic science, a branch of police work, uses scientific techniques to solve crimes. ____

1. Forensic detectives scientists who investigate crimes study murders that occurred long ago. ____
2. Bill Maples a forensic scientist tests corpses to find out if the deceased was murdered. ____
3. Zachary Taylor, the twelfth president of the United States, died of a mysterious stomach ailment in 1850. ____
4. Taylor may have been poisoned by political enemies, claims Clara Rising, a historical novelist. ____
5. Maples and other scientists looked for signs of arsenic a deadly poison in Taylor's body, but they didn't find any. ____
6. Maples was also asked to identify the skull and bones of Francisco Pizarro the Spanish conqueror of Peru. ____
7. A brutal ruler Pizarro was murdered by native Peruvians in 1541. ____
8. A forensic scientist James Starrs studied the murder of another American political figure from the past. ____
9. Huey Long U.S. senator and former governor of Louisiana was allegedly shot by a young man in 1935. ____
10. Tests by forensic scientists show that Carl Weiss a twenty-nine-year-old doctor may not have been the murderer after all. ____

**Name** ______________________ **Section** __________ **Date** __________

## ◆ 25.5 Using Commas to Set off Nonrestrictive Clauses

For help with this exercise, see section 25E in *Foundations First.* This exercise is also available online (Exercise Central, Chapter 25, 685).

Edit the following sentences for the correct use of commas to set off nonrestrictive clauses. Add commas where needed. If the sentence is correct, write *C* in the blank.

*Example:* Manatees, who are descended from a land animal, are closely related to elephants. ____

1. Manatees who are also known as sea cows are large mammals with flippers and a flat tail. ____

2. The huge creatures which often reach a length of ten feet and a weight of 800 to 1,000 pounds live in the warm waters of rivers, streams, and canals. ____

3. The peaceful plant eaters who have no natural enemies are in danger from people. ____

4. Motorboats, which can kill or seriously hurt manatees, threaten the survival of these animals. ____

5. Fishermen who dispose of fishing line in the water also endanger manatees. ____

6. Nylon fishing line, that manatees get caught in or swallow, can kill these animals. ____

7. The news that 325 manatees died in Florida in 2001 is not good for the survival of this species. ____

8. Florida which has a large population of manatees has declared them an endangered species. ____

9. Fortunately, groups that want to protect the manatee are helping keep these creatures safe. ____

10. Florida environmental groups have issued guidelines to boaters and fishermen which tell them how to avoid injuring manatees. ____

**Name** ______________________________ **Section** __________ **Date** __________

## ◆ 25.6 Using Commas in Compound and Complex Sentences

For help with this exercise, see section 25F in *Foundations First.* This exercise is also available online (Exercise Central, Chapter 25, 686).

Edit the following sentences for the correct use of commas in compound and complex sentences. Add commas where needed and take them out where they are not needed. If the sentence is correct, write *C* in the blank.

*Example:* Langston Hughes was a famous African-American writer, and was also a civil rights activist. ____

1. Langston Hughes was born in Joplin, Missouri, in 1902 and spent the first twelve years of his life in Lawrence, Kansas. ____
2. Neither his mother nor his father was able to raise him but his grandmother took on the job. ____
3. She taught him about his family's role in the fight to end slavery, and gave him a blood-stained shawl that once belonged to a hero killed in the struggle. ____
4. Langston loved his grandmother yet he was lonely. ____
5. The boy turned to books as his companions and he began to write poems at the age of thirteen. ____
6. When he was nineteen, Hughes won recognition with his poem entitled "The Negro Speaks of Rivers." ____
7. Hughes moved to New York City in the 1920s, and met other great African-American writers. ____
8. Langston Hughes wrote poetry, novels, short stories, plays, and children's books in which he showed his love for black people and black culture. ____
9. He had been a lonely child so it was important to him as an adult to have many friends. ____
10. Although some famous people become self-centered Langston Hughes always helped other writers. ____

Name ________________________________ Section ___________ Date ____________

## ◆ 25.7 Using Commas in Dates and Addresses

For help with this exercise, see section 25G in *Foundations First.* This exercise is also available online (Exercise Central, Chapter 25, 687).

Edit the following sentences for the correct use of commas in dates and addresses. Add any missing commas and cross out any unnecessary commas. If the sentence is correct, write *C* in the blank.

*Examples:* Mateo Solano was born on July 25, 1966. ____

Caracas, Venezuela, is his birthplace. ____

1. Mateo arrived in Berkeley California in 1986. ____
2. He shared an apartment at 1305 Cedar Street Berkeley with three other students from Venezuela. ____
3. Mateo graduated on June 21, 1988, from the University of California. ____
4. He married a young woman named Yolanda Ruiz on September 8 1990. ____
5. They both became American citizens on December 10, of that same year. ____
6. An important date for them was June 3, 1992, when their son was born. ____
7. The couple moved to Fort Lauderdale Florida when Mateo was offered an excellent job there. ____
8. They were able to buy a house at 58 Royal Palm Court, Boca Raton, a few months later. ____
9. Their first daughter was born on November 13, 1995, and the second one on May 16, 1997. ____
10. The couple will celebrate their fifteenth wedding anniversary on Thursday September 8, 2005 with a big party for family and friends. ____

Name ______________________ Section __________ Date __________

## ◆ 26.1 Using Apostrophes to Form Contractions

For help with this exercise, see section 26A in *Foundations First.* This exercise is also available online (Exercise Central, Chapter 26, 000).

Edit the following paragraph so that apostrophes are used correctly in contractions.

*Example:* Teachers and parents ~~shouldnt~~ shouldn't overlook the possibility that a child has a learning problem.

Just because a child has trouble learning to read doesnt mean he or she is slow or lazy. Often theyre hampered by a learning disability known as dyslexia. Dyslexic people dont see words on a page in the same way that other people do. They cant read because they see the letters in a word reversed. Theres a problem with the way their brains perceive print. However, these children arent unintelligent; most are very bright. Some dyslexics say its a blessing in disguise because they must find ways to compensate for their disability. One young man with this problem says, "The hardest experiences Ive faced have given me the greatest strength. I know Im smart. Youve got to work harder when you have dyslexia, but in the end, you can achieve more."

Name ____________________ Section __________ Date __________

## ◆ 26.2 Using Apostrophes to Form Possessives

For help with this exercise, see section 26B in *Foundations First.* This exercise is also available online (Exercise Central, Chapter 26, 000).

Rewrite the following groups of words, changing the singular or plural noun or indefinite pronoun that follows *of* to the possessive form.

*Example:* the boyfriend of Sis ____Sis's boyfriend____

1. the mascot of the team ____________________
2. the dresses of the girls ____________________
3. the health of your teeth ____________________
4. the sneakers of the men ____________________
5. the music of Alicia Keyes ____________________
6. the tails of the mice ____________________
7. the honking of the geese ____________________
8. the favorite of everyone ____________________
9. the survival of a species ____________________
10. the new car of the Joneses ____________________

Name ______________________ Section __________ Date __________

## ◆ 26.3 Avoiding Special Problems with Apostrophes

For help with this exercise, see section 26C in *Foundations First.* This exercise is also available online (Exercise Central, Chapter 26, 000).

In each of the following sentences, check the underlined words to be sure apostrophes are used correctly. If a correction needs to be made, cross out the word and write the correct version above it. If the noun or pronoun is correct, write *C* above it.

*Example:* Your [C] term paper is late, and ~~your~~ [you're] not even worried about it!

1. Each cat has it's own room in this luxury boarding house for cat's.
2. The red convertible is her's, but the blue station wagon is ours.
3. The police haven't figured out whose the murderer, but they know whose gun was used.
4. Its comforting to a puppy when it's mother is nearby.
5. Your looking wonderful since you're vacation in the Bahamas.
6. That problem is their's, and theres no reason for us to get involved.
7. The Gonzalezes' are good neighbors, and they're always willing to do a favor when we ask them.
8. I'm sorry I sat in your seat. I didn't realize it was your's.
9. Who's car is blocking our driveway, and who's going to call the police about it?
10. The girl's dormitory is on Madison Street, and it's not far from the school.

Name ______________________________ Section __________ Date __________

## ◆ 27.1 Capitalizing Proper Nouns

For help with this exercise, see section 27A in *Foundations First.* This exercise is also available online (Exercise Central, Chapter 27, 688).

Edit the following sentences, capitalizing letters and changing capitals to lowercase letters where necessary.

*Example:* When immigrants on a ship arrive in ~~n~~ew ~~y~~ork, the first thing they see is a famous ~~S~~tatue.
(N Y) (s)

1. The statue of liberty was a gift from the people of france to the people of the United States.

2. The gift was supposed to be presented on the Anniversary of the Founding of America, the fourth of July in 1876.

3. However, Frédéric-Auguste Bartholdi, the french Sculptor who designed the statue, couldn't get it finished on time.

4. He decided to send part of the sculpture of the woman called lady liberty, so that American Citizens could get an idea of what it would look like.

5. He sent the arm that holds the Torch to the Philadelphia world's fair in 1876.

6. The parts were huge since this would be the World's Biggest Statue at 216 feet tall.

7. The whole statue arrived at bedloe's island in New York harbor on June 17, 1885.

8. The giant statue had been taken apart for the trip across the atlantic ocean and packed in 214 boxes.

9. On october 18, 1886, president Grover Cleveland came to see the statue whose complete name is "liberty enlightening the world."

10. In 1903, a Poem by Emma Lazarus was engraved on a bronze tablet on the statue's Pedestal.

Name ______________________ Section __________ Date __________

## ◆ 27.2 Punctuating Direct Quotations

For help with this exercise, see section 27B in *Foundations First.* This exercise is also available online (Exercise Central, Chapter 27, 689).

In the following sentences containing direct quotations, first underline the identifying tag. Then punctuate the quotation correctly, adding capital letters where necessary.

*Example:* "Life is made up of sobs, sniffles, and smiles," said writer O. Henry, "with sniffles predominating."

1. The conductor said the next stop is Grand Central Station.
2. Why are you telling me all this Winona asked sharply.
3. If you are not telling me the whole truth the lawyer said I can't help you.
4. President Franklin D. Roosevelt told the American people the only thing we have to fear is fear itself.
5. If you can't stand the heat, get out of the kitchen said another U.S. president, Harry S. Truman.
6. Can you hand me that bread knife asked Pauline.
7. I'll lend you my lawn mower Pete replied if you take good care of it.
8. Don't touch that hot pan said the mother to the toddler.
9. Mark Twain remarked man is the only animal that blushes. Or needs to.
10. I thought I would get the part Bonnie complained but they gave it to someone else.

**Name** ______________________ **Section** __________ **Date** __________

## ◆ 27.3 Setting off Titles of Works

For help with this exercise, see section 27C in *Foundations First.* This exercise is also available online (Exercise Central, Chapter 27, 690).

In each of the following sentences, underline or insert quotation marks around titles. Correct all capitalization mistakes in titles.

*Example:* The song "Memories" became popular after it was featured in the Broadway musical <u>Cats</u>.

1. Laura Ingalls Wilder published her first novel, Little House in the Big Woods, when she was sixty-five years old.
2. Lawrence Durrell's essay Reflections on Travel appears in his book Spirit of Place.
3. People magazine has a feature called Where are they now? about the adult lives of child actors.
4. The Swimmer is one of the many humorous and moving short stories in The Stories of John Cheever.
5. The movie entitled The Sweet Hereafter was praised in a review in The New York Times.
6. The poem Kismet by Diane Ackerman is featured in The Art and Craft of Poetry by Michael Bugeja.
7. Although The Star-Spangled Banner is a popular American anthem, God Bless America is being sung more and more these days.
8. The episode of Frasier entitled The Proposal, in which Niles asks Daphne to marry him, was watched by millions of people.
9. Colonial Society is a chapter in the history textbook The American Past.
10. Our assignment is to read The Miller's Tale from Chaucer's The Canterbury Tales, an English classic written in verse.

Name ______________________________ Section __________ Date __________

## ◆ 28.1 Deciding between *ie* and *ei*

For help with this exercise, see sections 28A and 28B in *Foundations First*. This exercise is also available online (Exercise Central, Chapter 28, 691).

In each of the following sentences, proofread the underlined words for correct spelling. If a correction needs to be made, cross out the incorrect word and write the correct spelling above it. If the word is spelled correctly, write *C* above it.

*Example:* The children expressed ~~thier~~ (their) grief (C) over the cat's death by holding a funeral for it.

1. If Andy were to decieve anyone, his conscience would bother him.
2. In science, a researcher pays attention to his or her expereince of the physical world.
3. During ancient times, people beleived that the forces of nature were controlled by spirits.
4. All students' hieghts and wieghts were recorded on their medical charts.
5. When the nieghbors had some liesure time, they gathered to play card games, chess, and checkers.
6. Seize opportunities when they appear if you want to acheive your goals.
7. Foriegn students from eight countries are attending our college this year.
8. Neither of these paintings appeals to me, and I don't like the sculptures, either.
9. I haven't recieved word from my freind Rosa in a long time.
10. There's a wierd-looking spider crawling across the cieling.

Name ______________________ Section ____________ Date ____________

## ◆ 28.2 Understanding Prefixes

For help with this exercise, see section 28C in *Foundations First.* This exercise is also available online (Exercise Central, Chapter 28, 692).

Write in the blank the new word that results when the given prefix is added to each of the following words.

*Example:* un + believable = unbelievable

1. un + real = ____________________
2. over + done = ____________________
3. dis + approval = ____________________
4. non + fat = ____________________
5. co + ordinate = ____________________
6. bi + weekly = ____________________
7. re + make = ____________________
8. pre + view = ____________________
9. tele + marketing = ____________________
10. mis + understanding = ____________________

Name ______________________ Section __________ Date __________

## ◆ 28.3 Understanding Suffixes

For help with this exercise, see section 28D in *Foundations First*. This exercise is also available online (Exercise Central, Chapter 28, 693).

Fill in the blank by forming the word indicated in brackets. Make any spelling changes that are needed when the suffix is added to the given word.

*Example:* Some breeds of dogs are more ___easily___ trained than others. [easy + ly]

1. On February 11, 2002, some unusual dogs were _________ at the annual Westminster Dog Show at Madison Square Garden in New York City. [honor + ed]
2. These dogs—German shepherds, Labrador retrievers, and even some mutts—might not be beauties, but they are _________ champions. [true + ly]
3. They are search and rescue dogs who _________ to locate victims of the terrorist attacks on September 11, 2001. [try + ed]
4. Some of the dogs succeeded in _________ survivors trapped underneath the rubble of collapsed buildings. [rescue + ing]
5. Rescue workers then _________ the people out from under the debris. [pry + ed]
6. Many dogs and their trainers worked for twelve hours at a time in a _________ search for bodies of victims. [tire + less]
7. One dog, named Apollo, _________ at the World Trade Center just fifteen minutes after the towers collapsed. [arrive + ed]
8. Apollo was _________ surrounded by flames from falling debris and almost got burned. [complete + ly]
9. The applause that greeted the dogs and their trainers was a _________ tribute to these heroes. [fit + ing]
10. These heroic dogs were __________ in their orange coats with "Search and Rescue" written on them. [recognize + able]

Name ______________________ Section __________ Date __________

## ◆ 28.4 Understanding Suffixes

For help with this exercise, see section 28D in *Foundations First.* This exercise is also available online (Exercise Central, Chapter 28, 694).

Fill in the blank by forming the word indicated in brackets. Make any spelling changes that are needed when the suffix is added to the given word.

*Example:* The New York City firefighters acted in a ___heroic___ way during the September 11 disaster. [hero + ic]

1. Many stories of __________ have come out of the terrible events of September 11, 2001. [brave + ery]

2. The firefighters who rushed to the twin towers of the World Trade Center acted in a very __________ way. [courage + ous]

3. __________ their own safety, they supervised the evacuation of thousands of people. [Ignore + ing]

4. The brave firefighters kept __________ from floor to floor of the smoke-filled buildings. [move + ing]

5. __________ on each floor, they helped those lost in the smoke and confusion find the stairways. [Stop + ing]

6. They often had to make instant __________ about which was the safest route out of the building. [judge + ment + s]

7. Opening a door to a stairwell might mean __________ people in smoke or fire. [trap + ing]

8. Many firefighters __________ more than a hundred pounds of equipment, and some had to climb eighty flights of stairs that day. [carry + ed]

9. The firefighters' __________ to their duty to save people's lives impressed everyone. [dedicate + ion]

10. When more than three hundred firefighters were lost, the whole nation __________ mourned along with the heroes' families. [sincere + ly]

Name ______________________ Section __________ Date __________

## ◆ 29.1 Spelling Commonly Confused Words

For help with this exercise, see Chapter 29 in *Foundations First.* This exercise is also available online (Exercise Central, Chapter 29, 695).

Proofread the underlined words in the following sentences for correct spelling. If a correction needs to be made, cross out the incorrect word and write the correct spelling above it. If the word is spelled correctly, write *C* above it.

*Example:* "If you ~~brake~~ [break] that toy, I'm not going to buy [C] you another one!" the father said to the little boy.

1. Children are taught never to accept a peace of candy from a stranger.
2. Selena past the street she was looking for and had to fine her way back.
3. Having a conscious means being conscience of right and wrong.
4. Cliff was already to brake his car when the deer entered the road.
5. Nat was able to here everything the teacher said accept when the test would be given.
6. When a student feels nervous during a test, it can have a negative effect no matter how much he or she knows.
7. If I keep loose change in my pockets, I am likely to loose some of it.
8. Everyday, we hope for peace in the world.
9. I don't mine the noise; I don't let it effect me.
10. Mimi laid a blanket on the floor so the baby could lay on it.

Name ______________________________ Section ____________ Date ____________

## ◆ 29.2 Spelling Commonly Confused Words

For help with this exercise, see Chapter 29 in *Foundations First.* This exercise is also available online (Exercise Central, Chapter 29, 696).

Proofread the underlined words in the following sentences for correct spelling. If a correction needs to be made, cross out the incorrect word and write the correct spelling above it. If the word is spelled correctly, write *C* above it.

*Example:* The student asked the principal (C) to ~~right~~ (write) a recommendation for him on his college application.

1. We supposed that we would get a rise in our salaries, but we were wrong.
2. Stormy weather led the pilot to land the plain in a nearby field.
3. After moving from the city to the country, Tony found it hard to get use to the quite.
4. The outfielder through the ball right into the glove of the first baseman.
5. Brandy sit the vase of flowers on the table and than lit the candles.
6. Sumi wasn't sure weather or not to buy a use car.
7. Wayne said that he would rather be fired than go against his principles.
8. Go threw the tunnel and then turn left at the first traffic light.
9. Jason decided to quite smoking because he new it was a danger to his health.
10. The plane but beautiful chairs made by Shaker craftsmen are a pleasure to set on.

# Answers

### ◆ 9.1 Identifying Subjects

*Answers:* **1.** Every thirty-three years, the Tempel-Tuttle comet completes its orbit. **2.** Nearing the sun, it leaves a trail of dust particles behind. **3.** The earth passes through these trails each November. **4.** The earth's atmosphere then causes the dust particles to burn up. **5.** People on earth see these burning particles, or meteors, as streaks of light in the night sky. **6.** The meteors from Tempel-Tuttle's dust appear to come from the constellation Leo. **7.** Therefore, the annual November meteor shower is called the Leonid shower. **8.** In certain years, such as 2001, our traveling planet passes through several of Tempel-Tuttle's old trails in one evening. **9.** On November 18, 2001, some stargazers in North America saw as many as eight hundred meteors an hour during the Leonid shower. **10.** Appearing between 4 and 6 a.m. in most parts of the United States, the dazzling display caused many people to lose some sleep.

### ◆ 9.2 Recognizing Singular and Plural Subjects

*Answers:* **1.** A young person may be filled with doubts about going to college. *S* **2.** The college years bring about many changes in a person's life. *P* **3.** Many freshmen feel anxious about separating from their parents for the first time. *P* **4.** Career choices, social situations, relationships, and coursework all require attention from college students. *P* **5.** The fear of making bad decisions can paralyze some young people. *S* **6.** Depression is becoming fairly common among college students. *S* **7.** It can cause students to cut themselves off from other people and fail classes. *S* **8.** Many colleges and universities offer counseling services to their students. *P* **9.** A therapist can help a student adjust to college life. *S* **10.** A manageable level of stress is necessary for a successful college career. *S*

### ◆ 9.3 Identifying Subjects and Prepositional Phrases

*Answers:* **1.** Emperor penguins live only ~~in Antarctica~~. **2.** ~~Unlike most penguins~~, emperor penguins lay their eggs ~~during the dark, cold winter months~~. **3.** The female ~~of a penguin pair~~ lays a single egg. **4.** Afterward, she goes ~~to sea for two months~~ to find food. **5.** Held ~~between the male penguin's feet and his abdomen~~, the egg remains safe and warm. **6.** Male emperor penguins ~~with eggs~~ sleep ~~for twenty hours~~ a day, huddling together ~~for warmth during the incubation period~~. **7.** The males do not eat anything ~~for several weeks~~. **8.** Finally, the chicks hatch ~~in early spring~~. **9.** The mother penguins return to take care ~~of the chicks~~. **10.** Then the hungry fathers travel ~~to the ocean~~ to fatten themselves again.

### ◆ 9.4 Identifying Verbs

*Answers:* **1.** Babe Ruth, one of baseball's most popular players, held the record for home runs in a single season for thirty-four years. **2.** In 1961, Roger Maris set a new record over the objections of some fans. **3.** Maris, a shy, quiet man, hated attention from reporters and disliked the fame from his home-run record. **4.** Nevertheless, Maris's record lasted thirty-seven years. **5.** Mark McGwire shattered Maris's record of sixty-one home runs with seventy homers in 1998. **6.** Before the end of the 1998 season, McGwire visited the Maris family and won their support. **7.** Sportswriters looked again at Maris's accomplishments after McGwire's sixty-second home run that year. **8.** Maris's home-run record stayed on the books longer than any other record in baseball. **9.** McGwire's record, on the other hand, fell very quickly. **10.** In 2001, Barry Bonds outdid McGwire and established a new record of seventy-three home runs in a season.

## ◆ 9.5 Identifying Action and Linking Verbs

*Answers:* **1.** A company with low profits pressures managers to cut costs wherever possible. *AV* **2.** Employees often lose their jobs in a bad economy. *AV* **3.** In hard times, workers feel vulnerable to layoffs and cutbacks. *LV* **4.** As a business policy, a few companies refuse to lay off workers. *AV* **5.** They are eager to economize in other areas. *LV* **6.** Such companies become known for having loyal employees. *LV* **7.** Companies with no-layoff policies seem to many job-seekers to be ideal workplaces. *LV* **8.** However, these companies hire new employees rarely and cautiously. *AV* **9.** They also maintain the smallest possible workforce. *AV* **10.** Job security is difficult to find in both good economies and bad ones. *LV*

## ◆ 9.6 Identifying Main Verbs and Helping Verbs

*Answers:* **1.** Pet cats face many dangers outdoors. **2.** Thousands of them are killed by cars every year. **3.** Outdoor cats must also deal with other animals and with infectious diseases. **4.** In addition, cats can endanger backyard songbirds and small wildlife. **5.** There are many good reasons to keep pet cats inside the house. **6.** However, they may become obese and bored indoors. **7.** For several years, veterinarians have been recommending entertainment for indoor cats. **8.** Most cats enjoy the thrill of watching birds through a window or observing fish in an aquarium. **9.** Cats can even be trained to do tricks. **10.** A caring cat owner will make the cat happy in the house.

## ◆ 10.1 Forming Compound Sentences with Coordinating Conjunctions

*Answers:* **1.** Physical education in schools is essential, *for* it prepares children to be active and fit adults. **2.** Traditional physical education was supposed to interest children in athletic activities, *but/yet* too often only those who were already good athletes liked to participate. **3.** In traditional physical education classes, students played games well and enjoyed them, *or* they played them poorly and disliked them. **4.** Children who were not natural athletes often ended up hating physical education, *and* many of them never learned to enjoy physical activity, even as adults. **5.** Many Americans who do not get any exercise are obese, *and* obesity can cause many health problems. **6.** Fortunately, a new way of teaching physical education is becoming more common in American schools, *so* perhaps children in the future will have a different attitude toward physical activity. **7.** The new theory emphasizes fitness rather than athletic skill, *for* learning to keep fit benefits more children than learning to play a particular sport. **8.** A school gym of the future may contain weight machines, treadmills, and in-line skates, *so* children can participate in activities like the ones adults do at health clubs. **9.** The students will not be graded on how well they can play a sport, *but* they will be expected to work hard enough to keep their heart rate at a target level. **10.** This physical education plan would appeal to most educators, *and* many parents would also see the plan as a great improvement over the physical education classes of the past.

## ◆ 10.2 Forming Compound Sentences with Conjunctive Adverbs

*Suggested answers:* **1.** Laws in most states require people in the front seats of cars to wear seat belts; however, only a few states make rear-seat passengers wear safety belts. **2.** Rear-seat passengers who do not put on their seat belts can be seriously injured in an accident; moreover, they can hurt people in the front seat. **3.** In some states, people who were not wearing seat belts collect reduced damages if they are hurt in an accident; in other words, they must bear some of the financial responsibility for their injury. **4.** Any unrestrained person, animal, or thing in a car can be dangerous in an accident; therefore, car owners should look closely at everything they carry in the car. **5.** Storing loose objects in the trunk of the car is the best way to avoid danger; for example, putting a bag of groceries in the trunk prevents a can of soup from flying at a person's head after a sudden stop. **6.** Many SUVs and station wagons do not have trunks for storing luggage, groceries, and other items; instead, such vehicles have a storage space behind the passenger seats. **7.** Unrestrained objects can become projectiles and kill someone; therefore, car-safety specialists recommend cargo dividers or nets to prevent injury from objects in the backs of SUVs and station wagons. **8.** All states require young children to be buckled into a special car seat; consequently, injuries to young children in car accidents are less common than they were a decade ago. **9.** The law allows pets to roam freely in the car; nevertheless, animals can also suffer injuries or hurt someone else in an accident. **10.** Wearing a seat belt is sensible; in fact, not only front-seat passengers, but all people, animals, and objects are safer in a car when they are restrained.

## ◆ 11.1 Forming Complex Sentences with Subordinating Conjunctions

*Suggested answers:* **1.** *Since* he won a Tony Award for choreography for his work on the Broadway show *The Lion King*, Garth Fagan's name has been well known. **2.** The choreographer began as a dancer with a dance company in Jamaica, *where* he was born. **3.** As a young man, Fagan first studied with Ivy Baxter and other Caribbean dance teachers and performers *before* he moved to New York City to work with modern dancers like Martha Graham and Alvin Ailey. **4.** *After* he graduated from college in 1969, Fagan lived briefly in Detroit and then moved to Rochester, New York, to found his own dance company. **5.** Fagan then stopped dancing *so that* he could devote his attention to choreography and to instructing the fourteen members of the company, Garth Fagan Dance. **6.** Fagan chose untrained dancers for his troupe *because* he felt that he could more easily teach them his unique style of movement. **7.** *Although* Fagan's choreography is one of a kind, he acknowledges sources including modern dance, traditional Afro-Caribbean dance, and ballet. **8.** His African-inspired dances for *The Lion King* were seen by many more audiences *than* Fagan could attract in the relatively small world of dance performances. **9.** In addition to his enormous Broadway success, Fagan has continued to win prestigious prizes *wherever* he goes. **10.** *In order that* his dancers can share his success, he uses prize money to pay them good wages and offer them medical benefits.

## ◆ 11.2 Punctuating with Subordinating Conjunctions

*Answers:* **1.** Many people travel to winter carnivals in Rio de Janeiro and New Orleans because the parties are famously wild and the weather is warm in those cities. **2.** Whereas visitors to Rio and New Orleans are often seeking escape from the cold, the attractions at Quebec City's winter carnival emphasize ice and snow. **3.** Correct **4.** Although canoes are no longer essential for transportation in Quebec, the Carneval de Quebec honors tradition with canoe races across the St. Lawrence River. **5.** Sculptors come from all over the world so that they can compete in the ice-sculpting and snow-sculpting competitions held every year during the Carneval de Quebec. **6.** Correct **7.** Carnival visitors gasp as they stare at a palace made of seven hundred tons of ice **8.** Correct **9.** Correct **10.** Even though cognac breakfasts are no longer part of the winter carnival, children and grown-ups alike can still get a thrill from inner-tube sledding.

## ◆ 11.3 Forming Complex Sentences with Subordinating Conjunctions

*Suggested answers:* **1.** Parents should try to keep families together at mealtimes so that individual family members have an opportunity to talk and spend time together. **2.** Getting a family to eat meals together is a challenge in modern America even if the only problem is scheduling. **3.** Once someone in the family requires a special diet, the challenge of figuring out how to eat together becomes even more difficult. **4.** When some children discover where their meat comes from, they no longer want to eat meat. **5.** Although being a vegetarian may be a lifelong choice, it may also be a phase a child is going through. **6.** If the parent who prepares meals is not used to vegetarian cooking, a child's decision not to eat meat can cause conflicts. **7.** A vegetarian diet can be even healthier than a diet containing meat unless vegetarians limit their choices too strictly. **8.** Some parents prefer to begin cooking vegetarian meals for the whole family while a child wants to eat meatless meals. **9.** Other parents prepare two different meals for the family provided the children who will not eat meat are unable to cook their own preferred foods. **10.** Because food should unite families instead of dividing them, psychologists say that whenever possible, parents should not overreact by forcing children to eat food that they dislike.

## ◆ 11.4 Choosing the Correct Relative Pronoun

*Answers:* **1.** The education that Benjamin Franklin received in Boston schools ended when he was ten. (*that* describes *education.*) **2.** His older brother James, who ran a print shop, took Benjamin on as an apprentice. (*who* describes *James.*) **3.** Although he never returned to school, Franklin read every book that he could find. (*that* describes *book.*) **4.** He studied the British journal *The Spectator*, which taught him to write clearly and effectively. (*which* describes *The Spectator.*) **5.** After he quarreled with the brother who had given him the apprenticeship, Benjamin Franklin left Boston for Philadelphia. (*who* describes *brother.*) **6.** Franklin's formula for business success, which served him well as a printer and newspaper publisher, was to work harder than his competition. (*which* describes *formula.*) **7.** Franklin was also a pioneering scientist who conducted experiments with electricity. (*who* describes *scientist.*) **8.** Inventions that he created include bifocals and wood-burning stoves. (*that* describes *Inventions.*) **9.** Franklin was the only person to sign all four of the documents that ended the original colonies' ties with Great Britain and created the United States. (*that* describes *documents.*) **10.** At the end of his life, Franklin served as president of America's first antislavery society, which asked the U.S. Congress to abolish slavery. (*which* describes *society.*)

## ◆ 11.5 Recognizing Restrictive and Nonrestrictive Clauses

*Answers:* **1.** For many years, ulcers, which are irritated places on the stomach lining, have been attributed to stress. _*N*_ **2.** In 1982, physicians who had been studying ulcers discovered a different cause. _*R*_ **3.** Surprisingly, most ulcers are caused by a common bacterium that is called *H. pylori*. _*R*_ **4.** Patients whose symptoms were caused by *H. pylori* could be cured with antibiotics. _*R*_ [punctuation correct] **5.** However, stress, which has bad effects on health in other ways, may still have some responsibility for ulcers. _*N*_ **6.** Ulcers do not always strike people who have *H. pylori* in their systems. _*R*_ **7.** What is the trigger that causes the bacterium to create an ulcer? _*R*_ [punctuation correct] **8.** According to some scientists, stress may create conditions that allow *H. pylori* to cause an ulcer. _*R*_ **9.** Former prisoners of war, who have often suffered enough stress to be traumatized, are more likely to develop ulcers. _*N*_ **10.** A person's mental state, which may be positive or negative, can have an effect on health. _*N*_ [punctuation correct]

## ◆ 11.6 Forming Complex Sentences with Relative Pronouns

*Suggested answers:* **1.** Problems that come with an increasing world population include finding enough food for growing numbers of people. **2.** People around the globe rely on farmland, which has become increasingly productive in the past century, for their food. **3.** Today, a small farm that might have fed a single family in 1900 can produce more and better crops, thanks to fertilizers, pest controls, and other innovations. **4.** Farmers, who grow the crops to feed people all over the world, need water to have a successful harvest. **5.** Most of the scientists who study climate believe global warming is a reality. **6.** Global warming, which may cause only slight increases in world temperatures in the next century, can still disrupt rainfall patterns greatly. **7.** People who live in the Great Plains get much of their water from underground aquifers in that dry part of the United States. **8.** As less rain falls, people use more water from the aquifers, which will dry out in just a few decades at this rate of use. **9.** Other countries that have fast-growing populations and shrinking supplies of water face even more severe water shortages than the United States. **10.** A group of national leaders has met to discuss the world's water problem, which is likely to get worse before it gets better.

## ◆ 12.1 Varying Sentence Openings

*Possible answers:* **1.** Usually, manufacturers suggest a retail price that their products should carry. **2.** Retailers may, however, set any price that they like. **3.** In the consumer electronics field, sellers are very likely to set prices lower than the manufacturers suggest. **4.** Store prices are often two or three hundred dollars lower than the manufacturer's suggested retail price for items like digital cameras and big-screen televisions. **5.** In a recent study, consumers were asked whether they had paid full price for their latest electronics purchase. **6.** Surprisingly, seventy-five percent of the participants claimed to have gotten their merchandise on sale. **7.** Afterward, researchers wondered whether the terms *list price* and *sale price* have any meaning when so many people buy products "on sale." **8.** Manufacturers indeed seem to set their list prices artificially high. **9.** They can allow sellers to claim that their prices are twenty or forty percent lower than list price by doing this. **10.** In the end, consumers may not be hurt by the fact that so-called list prices are usually fictional, but the practice is not precisely honest.

## ◆ 12.2 Choosing Exact Words

Answers will vary.

## ◆ 12.3 Using Concise Language

*Suggested answers:* **1.** In 1893, Thomas Edison set up the original movie studio. **2.** The first films were silent because the technology for movies with sound did not exist. **3.** Early silent movies looked jumpy. **4.** The first silent films were also short, but studios later made full-length silents. **5.** Today, film scholars acknowledge that some silents were masterpieces. **6.** When making movies with sound became possible, the silents were doomed. **7.** An Al Jolson film in 1927 called *The Jazz Singer* was the first "talkie." **8.** Although silent movies were still popular, film studios decided that talking pictures and silent pictures could not both please moviegoers. **9.** Some studios released silent movies that played at the wrong speed to prevent audiences from enjoying them. **10.** The global popularity of silent films on television and at film festivals proves that the best silents can still attract audiences.

## ◆ 13.1 Recognizing Parallel Structure

*Answers:* **1.** The traditional foods of a culture remind people of their shared past and ~~are a way to~~ bind them together in the future. **2.** The foods of immigrants sometimes become part of the majority culture; Italian food and ~~eating~~ Chinese dishes have become popular all over the United States. **3.** A former empire may adopt food brought back from its colonies, as the Dutch love Indonesian restaurants and the British adore Indian ones. _P_ **4.** Sometimes, however, one culture's favorite foods leave people from other cultures uninterested or ~~they~~ even ~~feel~~ disgusted. **5.** For example, Marmite, a brown, salty, yeast-based spread, is a delicacy in England. _P_ **6.** Even Marmite's makers admit that the pungent odor of Marmite and *its* extremely strong *taste* offend some people. **7.** Around the world, foods like fermented eggs and insect larvae attract faithful devotees, passionate opponents, and very few *indifferent* diners ~~are indifferent to them~~. **8.** Regional foods in the United States are treasured in one area and ~~people have never~~ *un*heard of ~~them~~ elsewhere. **9.** New Yorkers eat knishes, Louisianans consume boudin, and Coloradans sample Rocky Mountain oysters. _P_ **10.** When people try to communicate across cultures, it is often easier at first to get to know others through their food than *to appreciate* ~~appreciating~~ different social customs.

## ◆ 13.2 Using Parallel Structure

*Suggested answers:* **1.** The first beauty pageants in the United States featured women wearing bathing suits and posing at the seaside. **2.** In the 1920s, many Americans felt that women who put themselves on display in a beauty contest were not moral, decent, and respectable. **3.** Many young women who participated in early Miss America contests wanted either to win a Hollywood film contract or to have a career on the stage. **4.** Lenora Slaughter, who was hired by Miss America pageant promoters in 1935, added a talent competition, persuaded society women to act as chaperones for the contestants, and convinced sponsors to offer the winners college scholarships. **5.** Bess Myerson, Miss America 1945, was not only the first scholarship winner but also the first Jewish Miss America. **6.** In the 1930s, pageant rules required contestants to be young, single, and white. **7.** Until the 1970s, neither the pageant's finalists nor any of the contestants were African American or Latina. **8.** Vanessa Williams's victory in 1983 was historic both because she was the first African-American winner and because she was the first winner to resign after a scandal. **9.** Williams may be the best-known Miss America, but she has made her name more as an actress and singer than as the winner of the Miss America pageant. **10.** Pageant promoters emphasize that Miss America must have brains and talent, but even brilliant contestants will not advance very far if they have extra pounds or unconventional looks.

## ◆ 14.1 Recognizing Run-ons and Comma Splices

*Answers:* **1.** We decided to get a dog last year, my sister wanted to get a puppy. *CS* **2.** My mother insisted on an adult dog she wanted to save an animal from a shelter. *RO* **3.** We adopted a seven-year-old dog from the local Humane Society. *C* **4.** The Humane Society officials were pleased few people want to adopt older dogs. *RO* **5.** Everyone at the Humane Society wished us well, they gave us tips on training our new pet. *CS* **6.** Fortunately, our dog was already housebroken that made owning him much easier. *RO* **7.** He did have some bad habits, such as jumping on visitors. *C* **8.** We signed him up for classes with a local dog trainer, the trainer helped us teach him better manners. *CS* **9.** Now our dog has been a part of the family for several months, we can hardly imagine life without him. *CS* **10.** A puppy might have been cuter however, this dog has a winning personality. *RO*

## ◆ 14.2 Correcting Run-ons and Comma Splices

*Possible answers:* **1.** The end of the football season in the United States is marked by the Super Bowl, which is the championship game between the winner of the American Football Conference and the winner of the National Football Conference. **2.** No football fan misses the big game; in addition, many people with little interest in football also turn on their televisions. **3.** The Super Bowl is famous for its advertisements. Many advertisers introduce new campaigns during the game. **4.** Advertisers pay top dollar for Super Bowl ad time, for they know that an enormous audience for their advertisements is guaranteed. **5.** While the Super Bowl often has higher ratings than any other television show of the year, even the shows that come on after the game attract record numbers of viewers. **6.** Super Bowl advertisements are often some of the best things on television. They may have cutting-edge technology or naughty humor. **7.** Many Americans have a Super Bowl tradition; usually, fans gather at someone's home to spend the afternoon eating, drinking, and watching the game. **8.** People attending a Super Bowl party expect certain kinds of food, and newspapers print Super Bowl party recipes for weeks before the game. **9.** Super Sunday promotions bombard Americans throughout the month of January as retailers offer specials on any item that can be linked to football. **10.** Although baseball is supposed to be America's national pastime, people witnessing Super Bowl hysteria must imagine that football is at least as popular.

## ◆ 15.1 Recognizing Sentence Fragments

*Answers:* **1.** The man behind Japanese animation was an illustrator. **2.** Named Osamu Tezuka. *F* **3.** He admired Disney animation. **4.** And created a comic book in 1951 about a robot child. *F* **5.** After the success of the comic book. *F* **6.** Tezuka turned it into an animated television show called *Astro Boy*. **7.** It attracted viewers all over the world. **8.** Japanese animated films and television programs are still hugely popular. **9.** With audiences in Japan. _F_ **10.** And are loved by growing numbers of people in America. _F_. The man behind Japanese animation was an illustrator named Osamu Tezuka. He admired Disney animation and created a comic book in 1951 about a robot child. After the success of the comic book, Tezuka turned it into an animated television show called *Astro Boy*. It attracted viewers all over the world. Japanese animated films and television programs are still hugely popular with audiences in Japan and are loved by growing numbers of people in America.

## ◆ 15.2 Correcting Phrase Fragments

*Answers:* **1.** Economic growth has been more important than clean air and water. **2.** In China for decades. **3.** Under the Kyoto Protocol. **4.** An agreement among industrialized and developing nations to decrease pollution and limit global warming. **5.** China will have to reduce carbon emissions from factories and cars. **6 .** Many supporters of the Kyoto agreement feared that China would resist changes. **7.** In the nation's environmental policy. **8.** According to Xie Zhenhua. **9.** The director of China's State Environmental Protection Administration. **10.** The Kyoto agreement will, in fact, benefit both the global environment and China's economy Economic growth has been more important than clean air and water in China for decades. Under the Kyoto Protocol, an agreement among industrialized and developing nations to decrease pollution and limit global warming, China will have to reduce carbon emissions from factories and cars. Many supporters of the Kyoto agreement feared that China would resist changes in the nation's environmental policy. According to Xie Zhenhua, the director of China's State Environmental Protection Administration, the Kyoto agreement will, in fact, benefit both the global environment and China's economy.

## ◆ 15.3 Correcting Incomplete Verbs

*Answers:* **1.** Melissa was expecting her first child last fall. **2.** She and her husband Julio have been married now for twelve years. **3.** Before their wedding, they had chosen not to have a baby right away. **4.** After five years of marriage, they were planning for a child. **5.** Melissa's mother had been hoping for a grandchild since the wedding. **6.** Julio's parents were not getting any younger, either. **7.** The pressure was making them very unhappy because they really wanted a baby. **8.** At last, in the spring of 2004, Melissa and Julio learned that they were going to have a daughter. **9.** They had never known such happiness before that day. **10.** Their baby girl is being treated like a princess by her parents and grandparents.

## ◆ 15.4 Correcting Dependent Clause Fragments

Answers will vary.

*Possible answers:* **1.** The car skidded across the intersection. **2.** A package had been left on the floor of the post office. **3.** My mother won't allow it. **4.** The woman hired his new boss. **5.** We realized what was happening. **6.** My brother works for a catering company. **7.** City officials refuse to discuss the power plant. **8.** The moon was full. **9.** The proposal will certainly be approved this month. **10.** The president made the speech.

## ◆ 16.1 Understanding Subject-Verb Agreement

*Answers:* **1.** shows **2.** tend **3.** contain **4.** wants **5.** expect **6.** use **7.** feels **8.** hopes **9.** starts **10.** need

## ◆ 16.2 Avoiding Agreement Problems with *Be, Have,* and *Do*

*Answers:* **1.** have **2.** does **3.** is **4.** has **5.** have **6.** do **7.** am **8.** are **9.** have **10.** do

## ◆ 16.3 Avoiding Agreement Problems with Compound Subjects

*Answers:* **1.** visit **2.** suggests **3.** live **4.** are **5.** swim **6.** are **7.** marks **8.** die **9.** remain **10.** is

## ◆ 16.4 Avoiding Agreement Problems When a Prepositional Phrase Comes between the Subject and the Verb

*Answers:* **1.** The skyline ~~of New York~~ (appears, appear) in many movies. **2.** The Empire State Building ~~on Thirty-Fourth Street~~ (remains, remain) a landmark. **3.** The twin towers ~~of the World Trade Center~~ (stands, stand) no longer at the foot of Manhattan. **4.** Residents ~~of the area~~ (misses, miss) the familiar sight. **5.** A controversy ~~over depictions of the twin towers~~ (exists, exist) among some filmmakers. **6.** Movies ~~in the city and elsewhere~~ (is, are) filmed long before their release to the public. **7.** A film ~~with New York settings~~ (is, are) often likely to contain footage of the missing towers. **8.** Many ~~of the directors~~ (wants, want) to remove the World Trade Center from their films. **9.** The sight ~~of the World Trade Center~~ (seems, seem) certain to distract moviegoers. **10.** However, New York views ~~with the empty skyline~~ (calls, call) attention to the towers' absence.

## ◆ 16.5 Avoiding Agreement Problems with Indefinite Nouns as Subjects

*Answers:* **1.** watches **2.** wants **3.** seems **4.** speaks **5.** makes **6.** is **7.** expects **8.** is **9.** offer **10.** has

## ◆ 16.6 Avoiding Agreement Problems When the Verb Comes before the Subject

*Answers:* **1.** There (is, are) more boys than girls with Asperger's syndrome. **2.** What (is, are) the symptoms of this condition? **3.** There (is, are) often an obsession with some subject. **4.** There (was, were) a boy in my kindergarten class fascinated by U.S. presidents. **5.** There (was, were) few other five-year-olds with such interests. **6.** There (has, have) been children obsessed with religion, too. **7.** How (does, do) parents cope with this syndrome? **8.** There (is, are) agreement among experts about the benefits of therapy. **9.** What (is, are) the prospects for a child with Asperger's syndrome? **10.** There (is, are) hope for a relatively normal life.

## ◆ 16.7 Avoiding Agreement Problems with *Who, Which,* and *That*

*Answers:* **1.** *visitors*. Summer visitors who (comes, come) to Grand Canyon National Park may be surprised by their experience. **2.** *overlook*. The Mather Point overlook, which (offers, offer) wonderful views of the canyon, can provide only sixty-five parking spaces. **3.** *cars*. On a summer day, more than a thousand cars that (arrives, arrive) at Mather Point must compete for those spaces. **4.** *tourists*. Tourists who (expects, expect) a serene view often get into fistfights. **5.** *rage*. The canyon's highways are not immune from the road rage that (is, are) found in other parts of the country. **6.** *people*. The people who (drives, drive) over 6000 cars to the Grand Canyon on an average summer day must hope to win one of the 2,400 parking spaces available. **7.** *problem*. Overcrowding is a problem that (has, have) concerned Park Service planners for over a decade. **8.** *railway*. A light railway that (was, were) supposed to limit the use of private cars inside the national park may not be built after all. **9.** *budget*. The park's budget, which (comes, come) from the federal government, ran into opponents in Congress. **10.** *station*. So far, no trains or tracks go to the Grand Canyon train station, which (was, were) completed in 2000.

## ◆ 17.1 Avoiding Illogical Shifts in Tense

*Answers:* **1.** Correct **2.** Hughes was born in Missouri and spent his first twelve years in Kansas. **3.** Although he is now associated with the Harlem Renaissance of the 1920s, he did not arrive in New York until 1921. **4.** At the time, he was nineteen years old. **5.** Hughes quickly made a name for himself with his poetry, publishing "The Negro Speaks of Rivers" in a national magazine that same year. **6.** Because he wanted only to write, not to teach or work in an office, Hughes tried nearly every kind of writing. **7.** Correct **8.** During his life, his poetry was very popular, and it is still widely read today. **9.** Correct **10.** Blue stone in the shape of a river decorates the floor of the auditorium, and an urn containing Hughes's ashes rests underneath the stone.

## ◆ 17.2 Avoiding Illogical Shifts in Person

*Answers:* **1.** My friend Sara works at a local historic house where people can take tours. **2.** Sara tells me terrible stories about her boss. **3.** The boss yells whenever she alters a single word of the speech that the visitors hear. **4.** Sara has won prizes at some of the public-speaking contests students can enter at school. **5.** She tries occasionally to give the visitors information about the house that they wouldn't ordinarily hear. **6.** However, the boss is only happy when she recites the memorized speech word for word. **7.** Recently, Sara was giving a tour to a group, and she could see that the mayor was one of the visitors. **8.** She told the group some things that she learned by working at the house—things that are not part of the speech. **9.** Her boss overheard, and she thought he was going to explode. **10.** Afterward, however, the mayor told Sara that she could apply to work as a summer assistant in the mayor's office and that she would be sure to remember Sara's name.

## ◆ 17.3 Avoiding Illogical Shifts in Voice

*Answers:* **1.** Martin drove his car too fast, and he received a speeding ticket. **2.** My sister checked out this book, but I read it. **3.** The landlord repaired the bathroom ceiling after the tenants reported a leak. **4.** Correct **5.** She gave up smoking because her mother was worried about it. **6.** Julie Andrews had a beautiful voice, but throat surgery stopped her singing career. **7.** My paper was nearly finished until my cat walked on my computer. **8.** The factory workers complained about conditions, but they did not join the union. **9.** Land mines injure hundreds of people every year, so she started a campaign to stop their use. **10.** The contestants jumped in a pool of sewage, and one of them won a lot of money.

## ◆ 18.1 Identifying Dangling Modifiers

*Answers:* **1.** <u>Offered a chance to go to college</u>, the diner seemed like a good way to earn some extra money. **2.** Correct **3.** <u>Settled in the back booth</u>, the jukebox blared a tune from the 1970s. **4.** <u>Avoiding the soup of the day</u>, grilled cheese sandwiches were a popular choice. **5.** <u>Leaving a very small tip</u>, the angry waiter tossed the coins on the floor. **6.** Correct **7.** Correct **8.** <u>Smoking in the restroom</u>, the fire alarms went off. **9.** <u>Emptied without warning</u>, one customer had just gotten his order. **10.** <u>Finding restaurant work a hard way to make a living</u>, the end of the shift could not come soon enough.

## ◆ 18.2 Correcting Dangling Modifiers

*Answers:* **1.** Buying tickets to the game in advance, we made plans for a night out. **2.** Fed and bathed, the children ate dinner early. **3.** Seeing our overheated car on the roadside, a passing motorist telephoned a mechanic. **4.** Arriving in a tow truck, the mechanic was playing the game on the radio. **5.** Watching the game on the garage's small television, we clearly showed our disappointment. **6.** Calling a taxi, the boss made arrangements to get us to the game. **7.** Driving too fast, the taxi attracted the attention of a police officer. **8.** Pitying our situation, the police officer sent us ahead on foot. **9.** Taking our tickets, the gatekeeper said that the game was half over. **10.** Forgetting everything that had happened on the way, we purchased hot dogs and drinks.

### ◆ 18.3 Identifying Misplaced Modifiers

*Answers:* **1.** Made of bricks, the third little pig felt safe in his [house]. **2.** With her big teeth, Red Riding Hood hardly recognized her [grandmother]. **3.** The [tortoise] defeated the hare in the race moving slowly and steadily. **4.** Correct **5.** [Cinderella] wept over missing the ball at the palace left behind in a ragged dress. **6.** Pinocchio's [nose] proved that he had told a lie growing longer every minute. **7.** Correct **8.** After rubbing the lamp three times, a genie appeared to [Aladdin]. **9.** Correct **10.** Lost and hungry, the gingerbread house looked delicious to [Hansel and Gretel].

### ◆ 18.4 Correcting Misplaced Modifiers

*Answers:* **1.** The plumber attempted to remove the debris clogging the drain. **2.** Full of energy, the chihuahua darted around the plumber's feet. **3.** The dog avoided the annoyed plumber waving a wrench. **4.** The hot water in the shower poured onto my head covered with shampoo. **5.** I yelled for the plumber cutting off the water main to stop. **6.** The plumber could not hear me over the chihuahua barking furiously. **7.** Shivering in the chilly shower stall, I waited for the water to come out of the faucet. **8.** With no knowledge of my predicament, the plumber went to get some lunch. **9.** Pulling on my robe and bunny slippers, I finally stormed out in search of the plumber. **10.** The chihuahua disappeared in front of my eyes filling with soap.

### ◆ 19.1 Using Regular Verbs in the Past Tense

*Answers:* **1.** approached **2.** rejected **3.** complained **4.** disappointed **5.** created **6.** changed **7.** earned **8.** lasted **9.** appeared **10.** succeeded

### ◆ 19.2 Using Irregular Verbs in the Past Tense

*Answers:* **1.** slept **2.** awoke **3.** threw **4.** drove **5.** found **6.** sprang **7.** chose **8.** thought **9.** spent **10.** left

### ◆ 19.3 Using the Past Tense of *Be*

*Answers:* **1.** was **2.** was **3.** was **4.** were **5.** was **6.** was **7.** were **8.** were **9.** were **10.** was

### ◆ 19.4 Using the Past Tense of *Can* and *Will*

*Answers:* **1.** can **2.** could **3.** would **4.** can **5.** will **6.** would **7.** could **8.** Would **9.** could **10.** would

### ◆ 20.1 Using Regular Past Participles

*Answers:* **1.** attended **2.** studied **3.** worked **4.** prepared **5.** cheated **6.** swallowed **7.** praised **8.** contributed **9.** insisted **10.** remained

### ◆ 20.2 Using Irregular Past Participles

*Answers:* **1.** led **2.** hurt **3.** chosen **4.** found **5.** slept **6.** gone **7.** awoken **8.** given **9.** taught **10.** kept

### ◆ 20.3 Using the Past and Present Perfect Tenses

*Answers:* **1.** wore **2.** listened **3.** hoped **4.** went **5.** has become **6.** has remained **7.** have become **8.** attended **9.** has collected **10.** has been

### ◆ 20.4 Using the Present Perfect and Past Perfect Tenses

*Answers:* **1.** had buried **2.** had maintained **3.** had proposed **4.** had kept **5.** had offered **6.** had sold **7.** had feared **8.** have promised **9.** have studied **10.** have awaited

### ◆ 20.5 Using the Past and Past Perfect Tenses

*Answers:* **1.** were **2.** had been **3.** had spent **4.** brought **5.** had given **6.** had occurred **7.** had poked **8.** were **9.** was **10.** had added

### ◆ 20.6 Using Past Participles as Adjectives

*Answers:* **1.** Baked **2.** broken **3.** Correct **4.** unconcerned **5.** Correct **6.** Correct **7.** worn **8.** alarmed **9.** Correct **10.** beaten

### ◆ 20.7 Using Past Participles as Adjectives

*Answers:* **1.** Bert served the roasted vegetables with rice. **2.** In this office, we keep confidential papers in a locked file cabinet **3.** Her mother repaired the child's torn dress. **4.** The licensed plumber knew how to fix the leaky pipe. **5.** Chilled white wine is often served with dessert. **6.** The determined protesters marched to the state capitol. **7.** Mr. Lopez is a certified teacher of mathematics. **8.** The unnoticed mistake was in the last paragraph. **9.** The lit candle quickly sputtered out. **10.** We opened our stuck door with a kick.

### ◆ 21.1 Forming Noun Plurals

*Answers:* **1.** Correct **2.** Correct, dishes **3.** daughters-in-law, wives **4.** loaves **5.** Correct, mixes, potatoes **6.** cousins, Correct, Correct **7.** Correct, people **8.** cries, babies **9.** speeches **10.** stories, Correct

### ◆ 22.1 Identifying Pronoun Antecedents

*Answers:* **1.** Elizabeth Cady Stanton **2.** women **3.** Elizabeth **4.** Elizabeth and Henry **5.** slavery **6.** women **7.** vote **8.** struggle **9.** a person opposed to votes for women **10.** women

### ◆ 22.2 Understanding Pronoun-Antecedent Agreement

*Answers:* **1.** they **2.** it **3.** he **4.** it **5.** him **6.** them **7.** them **8.** me **9.** his **10.** it

### ◆ 22.3 Understanding Pronoun-Antecedent Agreement with Compound Antecedents

*Answers:* **1.** they **2.** Correct **3.** he or she **4.** Correct **5.** they **6.** he or she **7.** them **8.** they **9.** Correct **10.** its

### ◆ 22.4 Understanding Pronoun-Antecedent Agreement with Indefinite Pronouns

*Answers:* **1.** pronoun: his or her; indefinite pronoun antecedent: *Each.* **2.** pronoun: his or her; indefinite pronoun antecedent: *Nobody.* **3.** pronoun: their; indefinite pronoun antecedent: *few.* **4.** pronoun: he or she; indefinite pronoun antecedent: *No one.* **5.** pronoun: its; indefinite pronoun antecedent: *Everything.* **6.** pronoun: his or her; indefinite pronoun antecedent: *Someone.* **7.** pronoun: his or her; indefinite pronoun antecedents: *Darlene, Stan.* **8.** pronoun: their; indefinite pronoun antecedent: *both.* **9.** pronoun: their; indefinite pronoun antecedent: *others.* **10.** pronoun: his or her; indefinite pronoun antecedent: *Another.*

### ◆ 22.5 Avoiding Vague Pronouns

*Answers:* **1.** My brother just got a job as a computer programmer at an insurance company. **2.** The instructions explained how to connect the television set and the VCR. **3.** The librarians in the school library provide lots of help with research. **4.** My aerobics instructor gives us a good workout. **5.** The Hershey, Pennsylvania, museum has an interesting exhibit about how chocolate is made. **6.** At the mall, the stores are having some terrific sales this weekend. **7.** The party that I was looking forward to turned out to be pretty boring. **8.** This sweater had a rip in it that I didn't notice when I bought it. **9.** The dog looks forward to his walk every day. **10.** On the radio, a reporter said that gasoline prices are going up.

### ◆ 22.6 Understanding Pronoun Case

*Answers:* **1.** He **2.** I **3.** me **4.** he **5.** us **6.** we **7.** me **8.** They **9.** them **10.** I

### ◆ 22.7 Understanding Pronoun Case: Compounds

*Answers:* **1.** me **2.** him **3.** He **4.** they **5.** she, I **6.** him **7.** They, I **8.** him, me **9.** him, her **10.** I

### ◆ 22.8 Understanding Pronoun Case: Comparisons

*Answers:* **1.** she [is] **2.** he [was] **3.** [it bothered] me **4.** I [do] **5.** [they frighten] us **6.** [it was for] them **7.** I [do] **8.** [it affected] her **9.** [it is costing] us **10.** I [do]

### ◆ 22.9 Understanding Pronoun Case: *Who, Whom*

*Answers:* **1.** who **2.** whom **3.** who **4.** whom **5.** who **6.** who **7.** who **8.** whom **9.** who **10.** who

### ◆ 22.10 Understanding Intensive and Reflexive Pronouns

*Answers:* **1.** herself **2.** themselves **3.** himself **4.** ourselves **5.** yourself **6.** myself **7.** himself **8.** itself **9.** herself **10.** yourselves

### ◆ 23.1 Using Adjectives and Adverbs

*Answers:* **1.** serious **2.** really **3.** destructive **4.** practically **5.** frequently **6.** evilly **7.** locally **8.** Nearly **9.** active **10.** unexpectedly

## ◆ 23.2 Using *Good* and *Well*

*Answers:* **1.** well **2.** good **3.** good **4.** well **5.** well **6.** good **7.** well **8.** well **9.** good **10.** well-

## ◆ 23.3 Using Comparatives and Superlatives

*Answers:* **1.** more idealistic **2.** stronger **3.** worst **4.** biggest **5.** more frightened **6.** greatest **7.** more upsetting **8.** scariest **9.** more determined **10.** happiest

## ◆ 23.4 Using the Comparative and Superlative of *Good/Well* and *Bad/Badly*

*Answers:* **1.** worst **2.** best **3.** better **4.** best **5.** better **6.** worse **7.** worst **8.** worse **9.** worse **10.** better

## ◆ 23.5 Using Demonstrative Adjectives

*Answers:* **1.** those **2.** those **3.** these **4.** these **5.** this, that **6.** those **7.** That, this **8.** these **9.** those **10.** this

## ◆ 24.1 Avoiding Special Problems with Subjects

*Answers:* **1.** I was surprised **2.** they don't **3.** They get milked **4.** It is an art **5.** Correct **6.** Correct **7.** Whey (It) is fed **8.** Goats **9.** they might be carrying **10.** names

## ◆ 24.2 Understanding Count and Noncount Nouns

*Answers:* **1.** noncount **2.** count, games **3.** noncount **4.** count, brains **5.** count, students **6.** noncount **7.** noncount **8.** count, diets **9.** count, tools **10.** noncount

## ◆ 24.3 Using Determiners with Count and Noncount Nouns

*Answers:* **1.** many **2.** a few **3.** these disabled **4.** much **5.** a few **6.** enough **7.** a few **8.** much **9.** each small **10.** little

## ◆ 24.4 Understanding Articles

*Answers:* **1.** the, no article **2.** no article **3.** an, a, no article, no article **4.** the, a **5.** an **6.** the, no article **7.** an **8.** the, a **9.** a, no article **10.** an, a, the

## ◆ 24.5 Forming Negative Statements and Questions

*Answers:* **1.** Erin has not finished her term paper. **2.** The musicians are not playing love songs. **3.** The buses do not leave the terminal every hour. **4.** She did not look under the bed for her missing shoe. **5.** They did not worry about missing the train. **6.** Jed did not find the stock certificates in the desk. **7.** Dinner will not be served in the main dining hall. **8.** Hashim has not been absent for a week. **9.** Lahela did not feel proud of winning the swim event. **10.** Iliana will not meet us at the movie theater.

## ◆ 24.6 Recognizing Stative Verbs

*Answers:* **1.** verb: has been writing; correct **2.** verb: is loving; loves **3.** verb: has been expressing; correct **4.** verb: are liking; like **5.** verb: are wanting; want **6.** verb: are being;

are **7.** verb: are arguing; argue **8.** verb: is becoming; correct **9.** verb: is believing; believes **10.** verb: is understanding; understands

## ◆ 24.7 Placing Adjectives in Order

*Answers:* **1.** some annoying, impatient customers **2.** this silly, sentimental love song **3.** an ugly green wool coat **4.** a charming little country cottage **5.** these talented young rock musicians **6.** Juanita's lovely, colorful flower paintings **7.** my sweet, fluffy white cat **8.** all the best possible excuses **9.** her sister's expensive blue cashmere sweater **10.** both mischievous, dirt-covered twin boys

## ◆ 24.8 Using Prepositions Correctly

*Answers:* **1.** from, on, to **2.** in **3.** to, in **4.** no prepositions **5.** by, in **6.** of, in, about **7.** from, of **8.** of, on **9.** on **10.** in, of **11.** at, under

## ◆ 25.1 Using Commas in a Series

*Answers:* **1.** We ordered a pizza with pepperoni, mushrooms, anchovies, and extra cheese. **2.** Correct **3.** Ginny is cooking the main dish, Bruce is making the salad, and the twins are setting the table. **4.** Three movies set in New York City are *Taxi Driver, Wall Street,* and *The Godfather.* **5.** Correct **6.** They brought food, water, mosquito repellent, sunscreen, a compass, and a map along on the hike. **7.** Bob collected the money at the door, Tara showed the audience members to their seats, and Vinnie acted as master of ceremonies. **8.** Marissa pinned on the pattern and cut the cloth and sewed the skirt in under an hour. **9.** We can take a bus, a train, or a cab to the airport. **10.** Correct

## ◆ 25.2 Using Commas to Set off Introductory Phrases

*Answers:* **1.** During the Bolshevik (Communist) Revolution, the Russian czar (ruler) and his family were murdered. **2.** On the night of July 17, 1918, the royal family was awakened by soldiers of the revolutionary army. **3.** Along with their private doctor and some servants, the family was taken to the basement of a house in which they were staying. **4.** Correct **5.** According to historians, two of the bodies were burned, and the other nine were buried. **6.** Many years later, a woman claimed to be Princess Anastasia, who was seventeen at the time of the murders. **7.** Telling a complicated story, the woman insisted that she had been shot but survived. **8.** Correct **9.** In spite of her efforts, they didn't believe her story because she could not speak Russian. **10.** At the present time, Anastasia's body still has not been found.

## ◆ 25.3 Using Commas to Set off Parenthetical Words and Phrases

*Answers:* **1.** Lance, where did you leave the car keys? **2.** We can, however, just stay home and have a quiet evening. **3.** Instead, I'd rather use the money for a vacation. **4.** Correct **5.** However, I hope I don't have to go there again for a long time. **6.** Celine Dion, for example, achieved success as a singer at an early age. **7.** How did you catch the criminal, Sherlock Holmes? **8.** I hope you realize, moreover, that this is your last chance. **9.** Correct **10.** Consequently, his grades began to slide.

## ◆ 25.4 Using Commas with Appositives

*Answers:* **1.** Forensic detectives, scientists who investigate crimes, study murders that occurred long ago. **2.** Bill Maples, a forensic scientist, tests corpses to find out if the deceased was murdered. **3.** Correct **4.** Correct **5.** Maples and other scientists looked for signs of arsenic, a deadly poison, in Taylor's body, but they didn't find any. **6.** Maples was also asked to identify the skull and bones of Francisco Pizarro, the Spanish conqueror of Peru. **7.** A brutal ruler, Pizarro was murdered by native Peruvians in 1541. **8.** A forensic scientist, James Starrs, studied the murder of another American political figure from the past. **9.** Huey Long, U.S. senator and former governor of Louisiana, was allegedly shot by a young man in 1935. **10.** Tests by forensic scientists show that Carl Weiss, a twenty-nine-year-old doctor, may not have been the murderer after all.

## ◆ 25.5 Using Commas to Set off Nonrestrictive Clauses

*Answers:* **1.** Manatees, who are also known as sea cows, are large mammals with flippers and a flat tail. **2.** The huge creatures, which often reach a length of ten feet and a weight of 800 to 1,000 pounds, live in the warm waters of rivers, streams, and canals. **3.** The peaceful plant eaters, who have no natural enemies, are in danger from people. **4.** Correct **5.** Correct **6.** Nylon fishing line that manatees get caught in or swallow can kill these animals. **7.** Correct **8.** Florida, which has a large population of manatees, has declared them an endangered species. **9.** Correct **10.** Florida environmental groups have issued guidelines to boaters and fishermen, which tell them how to avoid injuring manatees.

## ◆ 25.6 Using Commas in Compound and Complex Sentences

*Answers:* **1.** Correct **2.** Insert comma after *him* **3.** Delete comma after *slavery* **4.** Insert comma after *grandmother* **5.** Insert comma after *companions* **6.** Correct **7.** Delete comma after *1920s* **8.** Correct **9.** Insert comma after *child* **10.** Insert comma after *self-centered*

## ◆ 25.7 Using Commas in Dates and Addresses

*Answers:* **1.** Mateo arrived in Berkeley, California, in 1986. **2.** He shared an apartment at 1305 Cedar Street, Berkeley, with three other students from Venezuela. **3.** Correct **4.** He married a young woman named Yolanda Ruiz on September 8, 1990. **5.** They both became American citizens on December 10 of that same year. **6.** Correct **7.** The couple moved to Fort Lauderdale, Florida, when Mateo was offered an excellent job there. **8.** Correct **9.** Correct **10.** The couple will celebrate their fifteenth wedding anniversary on Thursday, September 8, 2005, with a big party for family and friends.

## ◆ 26.1 Using Apostrophes to Form Contractions

*Answers:* Just because a child has trouble learning to read *doesn't* mean he or she is slow or lazy. Often *they're* hampered by a learning disability known as dyslexia. Dyslexic people *don't* see words on a page in the same way that other people do. They *can't* read because they see the letters in a word reversed. *There's* a problem with the way their brains perceive print. However, these children *aren't* unintelligent; most are very bright. Some dyslexics say *it's* a blessing in disguise because they must find ways to compensate for their disability. One young man with this problem says, "The hardest experiences *I've* faced have given me the greatest strength. I know *I'm* smart. *You've* got to work harder when you have dyslexia, but in the end, you can achieve more."

## ◆ 26.2 Using Apostrophes to Form Possessives

*Answers:* **1.** the team's mascot **2.** the girls' dresses **3.** your teeth's health **4.** the men's sneakers **5.** Alicia Keyes's music **6.** the mice's tails **7.** the geese's honking **8.** everyone's favorite **9.** a species's survival **10.** the Joneses' new car

## ◆ 26.3 Avoiding Special Problems with Apostrophes

*Answers:* **1.** its; cats. **2.** hers; correct **3.** who's; correct **4.** It's; its **5.** You're; your **6.** theirs; there's **7.** Gonzalezes; correct **8.** correct; yours **9.** Whose; correct **10.** girls'; correct

## ◆ 27.1 Capitalizing Proper Nouns

*Answers:* **1.** Statue; Liberty; France **2.** anniversary; founding; Fourth **3.** French; sculptor **4.** Lady; Liberty; citizens **5.** torch; World's; Fair **6.** world's; biggest; statue **7.** Bedloe's; Island; Harbor **8.** Atlantic; Ocean **9.** October; President; Liberty; Enlightening; World **10.** poem; pedestal

## ◆ 27.2 Punctuating Direct Quotations

*Answers:* **1.** The conductor said, "The next stop is Grand Central Station." **2.** "Why are you telling me all this?" Winona asked sharply. **3.** "If you are not telling me the whole truth," the lawyer said, "I can't help you." **4.** President Franklin D. Roosevelt told the American people, "The only thing we have to fear is fear itself." **5.** "If you can't stand the heat, get out of the kitchen," said another U.S. president, Harry S. Truman. **6.** "Can you hand me that bread knife?" asked Pauline. **7.** "I'll lend you my lawn mower," Pete replied, "if you take good care of it." **8.** "Don't touch that hot pan!" said the mother to the toddler. **9.** Mark Twain remarked, "Man is the only animal that blushes. Or needs to." **10.** "I thought I would get the part," Bonnie complained, "but they gave it to someone else."

## ◆ 27.3 Setting off Titles of Works

*Answers:* **1.** Laura Ingalls Wilder published her first book, Little House in the Big Woods, when she was sixty-five years old. **2.** Lawrence Durrell's essay "Reflections on Travel" appears in his book Spirit of Place. **3.** People magazine has a feature called "Where Are They Now?" about the adult lives of child actors. **4.** "The Swimmer" is one of the many humorous and moving short stories in The Stories of John Cheever. **5.** The movie entitled The Sweet Hereafter was praised in a review in The New York Times. **6.** The poem "Kismet" by Diane Ackerman is featured in The Art and Craft of Poetry by Michael Bugeja. **7.** Although "The Star-Spangled Banner" is a popular American anthem, "God Bless America" is being sung more and more these days. **8.** The episode of Frasier entitled "The Proposal," in which Niles asks Daphne to marry him, was watched by millions of people. **9.** "Colonial Society" is a chapter in the history textbook The American Past. **10.** Our assignment is to read "The Miller's Tale" from Chaucer's The Canterbury Tales, an English classic written in verse.

## ◆ 28.1 Deciding between *ie* and *ei*

*Answers:* **1.** deceive; correct **2.** correct; experience **3.** correct; believed **4.** heights; weights **5.** neighbors; leisure **6.** seize; achieve **7.** Foreign; correct **8.** Correct; correct **9.** received; friend **10.** weird; ceiling

## ◆ 28.2 Understanding Prefixes

*Answers:* **1.** un + real = *unreal* **2.** over + done = *overdone* **3.** dis + approval = *disapproval* **4.** non + fat = *nonfat* **5.** co + ordinate = *coordinate* **6.** bi + weekly = *biweekly* **7.** re + make = *remake* **8.** pre + view = *preview* **9.** tele + marketing = *telemarketing* **10.** mis + understanding = *misunderstanding*

### ◆ 28.3 Understanding Suffixes

*Answers:* **1.** honored **2.** truly **3.** tried **4.** rescuing **5.** pried **6.** tireless **7.** arrived **8.** completely **9.** fitting **10.** recognizable

### ◆ 28.4 Understanding Suffixes

*Answers:* **1.** bravery **2.** courageous **3.** Ignoring **4.** moving **5.** Stopping **6.** judgments **7.** trapping **8.** carried **9.** dedication **10.** sincerely

### ◆ 29.1 Spelling Commonly Confused Words

*Answers:* **1.** Correct, piece **2.** passed, find **3.** conscience, conscious **4.** all ready, Correct **5.** hear, except **6.** Correct, Correct **7.** Correct, lose **8.** Every day, Correct **9.** mind, affect **10.** Correct, lie

### ◆ 29.2 Spelling Commonly Confused Words

*Answers:* **1.** Correct, raise **2.** Correct, plane **3.** used, quiet **4.** threw, Correct **5.** set, then **6.** whether, used **7.** Correct, Correct **8.** through, Correct **9.** quit, knew **10.** plain, sit